G000244357

RAILWAY DEPOTS

Paul Smith and Philip Stuart

PUBLISHING

THIS BOOK IS DEDICATED TO THE MEMORY OF
SHIRLEY ANN SMITH
(27 July 1942 - 25 July 2007)
and
ALLAN SOMMERFIELD
(2 January 1934 - 4 November 2009)

RAIL ENTHUSIASTS, AUTHORS AND MEMBERS OF THE ENGINE SHED SOCIETY

First pub' hed 2010

ISBN 978 0 7110 3482 2

© Ian Allan Publishing Ltd 2010

Published by Ian Allan Publishing
an imprint of Ian Allan Publishing Ltd, Hersham, Surrey, KT12 4RG
Printed in England by Ian Allan Printing Ltd, Hersham, Surrey, KT12 4RG

Code: 1006/x

Distributed in Canada and the United States of America by BookMasters Distribution Services

Visit the Ian Allan Publishing website at www.ianallanpublishing.com

Front cover: GBRf Class 66 locomotives Nos 66 730, 66 711 and 66 701 parked outside of
Peterborough New England depot on 22 October 2008. *Nick Pigott*

Back cover: Northampton Kings Heath depot on 27 June 2006. *Chris Milner*

Previous page: Carlisle Kingmoor depot on 11 July 2009 with Nos 37 229, 37 081, 47 739 *Colas,*
50 049, 66 412 and 66 411 on shed. *Richard Gennis*

Above: Class 37s Nos 37 229, 37 609 and 37 423 in the shed yard at Gresty Bridge depot on
19 July 2008. *Richard Gennis*

INTRODUCTION

DEPOT DIRECTORIES, 1947 AND 2010

The British Locomotive Shed Directory was first published on the eve of railway nationalisation, so a 21st-century successor has to take account of more than 60 years of technological and organisational developments. What has changed? What, if anything, remains the same?

The elimination of steam occasioned the most important change in the nature of motive power depots. Whereas diesels and electrics can simply be switched on or off at the start or end of a duty and left in any convenient siding, a steam locomotive needs several hours of preparation before working and proper disposal afterwards. Taking on coal and water and discharging ash effectively meant spending several hours of every working day on shed. In contrast refuelling diesels needs nothing more than a stabling point with access for a road tanker. All forms of traction need depots for regular inspection and maintenance, but the steam-age practice of sending locomotives to Works for major overhauls became unnecessary when such components as traction motors, bogies and even power units could be exchanged in the course of normal maintenance. As depots acquired lifting jacks, wheel-lathes and, in some cases, paint shops then those Works that survived found their role largely confined to new builds, major refurbishments and accident damage repairs.

The privatisation of our railway system has led to a great transformation in the way that it is operated, and the provision of depots has not been immune from this. During the changeover from steam to diesel the obvious policy was to provide large locomotive sheds across the country, but the demise of locomotive-hauled passenger trains and the fragmentation of locomotive stock has all but wiped out these huge depots. Only DB Schenker's Toton, Knottingley and DRS's rebuilt and re-opened Kingmoor currently survive, whilst famous names such as Tinsley and Stratford have disappeared without trace. In their stead has come an expansion of maintenance and servicing facilities for EMU and DMU stock and a number of small locomotive depots, some converted from wagon works or goods sheds.

Steam locomotive depots were complemented by carriage sheds, which the Directory did not deign to notice. Some of them latterly housed the multiple-units that soon monopolised rural and suburban passenger services, though diesel and electric locomotives shared inter-city services with HSTs for many years. Nowadays a Directory confined to locomotive depots would be a slim volume indeed and virtually limited to freight haulage. Most of the post-privatisation multiple-unit fleets have been allocated to newly built depots, with their manufacturers taking on long-term responsibility for maintenance. Yet if depots like Bombardier's Central Rivers (2001) appear to represent the most radical departure from the engine sheds of 60 years ago, it is worth remembering that the Southern Railway opened numerous electric multiple-unit depots in the 1930s which, though modernised and re-clad, continue in use today.

Another aspect of the advent of diesels was the introduction of self-propelled track maintenance machines and buildings in which to service them. Since privatisation some companies have had interests in both permanent-way maintenance and freight haulage and, in consequence, a number of permanent-way depots have seen intermittent use as locomotive fuelling and servicing points.

Given the contraction of the network, the location of depots has changed less than might be expected. The sub-shed found at almost every branch-line terminus has long gone, but the sites of around 80% of BR's coded sheds are as visible from passing trains as they ever were, whilst only some 6% are, like Brecon, remote from any railhead. Many purpose-built diesel and electric depots are on, or adjacent to, the sites of steam sheds; few are more than two or three miles from a site listed in the original Directory.

3

CRITERIA FOR INCLUSION
DEPOTS

For present purposes a depot is defined as a main-line site with a building entered by locomotives or powered passenger rolling stock for fuelling, servicing or maintenance. For locomotives this can range from a major facility such as Toton to a tiny fuelling shelter such as Mountsorrel, just as the original Directory ranged from Old Oak Common to Dowlais Central. A feature of the current railway landscape is the suddenness with which depots are either opened or closed. In 2009 the example of Advenza, a company that had scarcely advented before it was gone again, highlights the difficulty of whether to list or omit a depot or SP that may have closed or re-opened whilst this survey was going to press. In view of this some of the locomotive depots that were unused at the start of 2010, and could easily be re-opened, have been included.

For multiple-units the criteria can include a site equipped with lifting jacks and a wheel lathe, or one limited to just carriage cleaning. The definition excludes wagon repair shops and permanent-way depots, unless sharing their facilities with locomotives, and major workshops. As the original Directory included both locomotive sheds and works it is worth noting that the only survivors of the latter are Crewe, Eastleigh and Glasgow Springburn, plus part of the former Railway Technical Centre at Derby. Of the many private locomotive building workshops, only Brush at Loughborough remains. Former BR carriage works still operating are Derby Litchurch Lane, Doncaster, Eastleigh, Glasgow Springburn, and Wolverton plus the heavy repair shop at Chart Leacon (1961) and the Hunslet-Barclay works at Kilmarnock (1991).

The transfer of the East London Line from London Underground to London Overground adds its new depot at New Cross Gate to the list, whilst the BR multiple-unit facility at South Gosforth dropped out when transferred to the Tyne & Wear Metro. Privatisation blurred the distinction between the main-line railway and the independent heritage lines so that some sites primarily concerned with restoration and preservation have the facilities to maintain locomotives for spot-hire main-line use, and accordingly qualify for inclusion. Two new depots, at Hornsey and Three Bridges, were due to be constructed and opened in 2010 for Thameslink EMUs.

STABLING POINTS (SPs)

A section at the end of this volume deals with some of the locomotive stabling points effectively open-air fuelling points or train crew depots, where locomotives await their next duty. Similar facilities for multiple-units, ranging from station sidings to extensive sites with offices, cleaning plants and washers, such as at Shoeburyness and Yoker, are not covered.

Competition between freight companies has meant that, as contracts to operate particular services are won and lost, arrangements for servicing locomotives at convenient points *en route* can result in short-term use of a location.

VISITING THE DEPOTS

One issue, trespass, remains unchanged in the letter but transformed in the spirit. The 1947 Directory asserted in bold capitals that 'IT IN NO WAY GIVES AUTHORITY TO ENTER THESE PLACES', and that is equally true of this publication. But everyone knew that the Directory was in effect a shed-basher's bible. Few depots were seriously bothered by the regular incursion of youthful spotters, and being seen off the premises by an irate foreman was the worst to be expected. Not any more! Thanks to a combination of Health & Safety legislation, the threat of terrorist attacks on public transport and the fashion amongst teenagers for covering rolling stock with graffiti instead of writing numbers in notebooks, most depots now have palisade fencing, electronically controlled gates, CCTV and security guards. A few depots hold occasional open days, but as for unauthorised visits — don't even think about it!

NOTES ON THE USE OF THIS BOOK

A page has been allotted to each depot and the information includes:

Address and postcode: where possible we have endeavoured to obtain the official versions but where these have not been available the nearest postcode to the depot entrance has been sourced.

Maps: the simplified maps are drawn to a scale of 7.8in : 1 mile. Railway lines = black, A roads = red, B and other roads = orange, Motorways = blue, Waterways = azure, Depot buildings = dark green, Museum and preservation sites = magenta.

Walking directions from nearest railway station: in all instances the approximate distances quoted relate to those to the depot entrance.

History and description:

Notes: T = track; with steam sheds TS means track straighthouse.

To distinguish between the original London & North Western Railway and the current one, the former is identified as LNWR and the latter as L&NWR.

ACKNOWLEDGEMENTS

The authors would like to thank the following for their generous supply of photographs and information: Mervyn Allcock, Keith Batchelor, Tony Booth, Roger Butcher, Richard Gennis, Roger Griffiths, John Groocock, John Hillmer, Paul Jordan, Dave McGuire, Chris Milner, Brian Morrison, Nick Pigott, Allison Smith, the late Allan Sommerfield, Peter Waller and Edward Watts.

CINDER PATH? ......WHAT CINDER PATH?

Many steam sheds had no road access, and readers familiar with the old Directory will fondly recall its familiar conclusion: 'A cinder path leads to the shed', a path that often afforded a good view of the yard before reaching the office. But by 2005 a notice proclaiming 'All Visitors Report to Security Cabin. All I.D. To be Shown to Security Prior to Entry' was the sign of changed times at Selhurst depot.
Philip Stuart

ABERDEEN CLAYHILLS

Clayhills Depot, South College Street, Aberdeen AB11 6JW

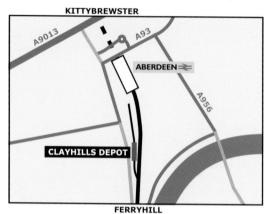

The yard is visible from the line

> **Directions from Aberdeen station:**
> Turn left along Guild Street, left into College Street, continue into South College Street and the depot entrance is on the left.
> (Distance approx 700yd)

A 1T through-road shed located at NJ94200543 and constructed in brick and corrugated sheeting with a single-pitched roof clad in corrugated sheeting. It was opened in 1987 by BR Inter-City to replace the depot at Aberdeen Ferryhill, and in 2010 was in use to service HSTs and the 'Caledonian Sleeper'.
Operating company in 2010: First Scotrail
Allocation: None

The north end of Aberdeen Clayhills depot, viewed on 1 August 1989. Although not visible Class 08 0-6-0 No 08 855 was stabled inside the building. *Philip Stuart*

ASHFORD

Ashford Maintenance Centre, Station Approach, Ashford TN23 1EZ

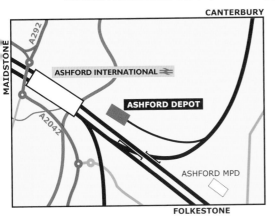

The yard is visible from the lines

Directions from Ashford International station:
Leave via the exit on the down side and the depot entrance is on the right, adjacent to the station car park.
(Distance approx 100yd)

A 5T dead-ended shed, located at TR01644200 and constructed in brick and sheeting on a steel frame with a sheeting-clad and glazed shallow Dutch barn-style roof. It occupies the site of former sidings and a diesel SP and was officially opened by Hitachi Rail Maintenance (UK) Ltd on 2 October 2007.
Operating company in 2010: Hitachi
Allocation: Home base for Class 395 fleet

Ashford depot on official opening day — 2 October 2007.

Nick Pigott

AYLESBURY

Chiltern Railways, Leach Road, Aylesbury HP21 8XJ

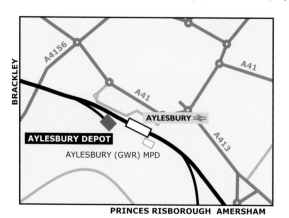

The yard is visible from the line

> **Directions from Aylesbury station:**
> Turn left outside of the station, go over the bridge and the depot entrance is on the right.
> (Distance approx 200yd)

A 3T dead-ended shed, with one through road, constructed in brick and corrugated sheeting on steel frames with a flat corrugated sheeting-clad roof located at SP81641347 and adjoined on the east side by a 1T through-road fuelling shed. The depot was opened on 14 May 1991 by Network SouthEast as a replacement for Marylebone depot when 'Networker' units supplanted DMUs. It was transferred to Adtranz, for Chiltern Railways, on 15 September 1996 and taken over by Bombardier in 2000. By 2005 the depot had been extended with an additional 1T dead-ended shed on the east side.

Operating company in 2010: Bombardier for Chiltern Railways
Allocation: Home base for Class 165 and 168 fleets

Aylesbury depot viewed from the north west on 20 September 2008 and showing the 2005 extension on the east side.
Philip Stuart

AYR
Tryfield Place, Ayr KA8 8HH

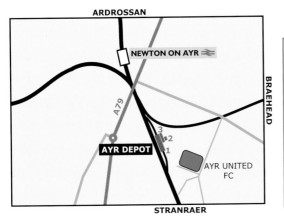

The yard is visible from the line

Directions from Newton-on-Ayr station: Go straight ahead along Falkland Park Road, turn right along Prestwick Road and left into McCall's Avenue. Turn right into Somerset Road and right after Ayr United FC's ground into Tryfield Place. The depot is at the end of this road.
(Distance approx 0.6 miles)

Building 1: This site has been in use for locomotive maintenance and servicing since the Glasgow & South Western Railway opened a stone-built 6TS through-road shed with a twin gable-style roof here in 1879. It was employed solely as a steam depot until 1959 when the westernmost portion of the building, located at NS34292275, was provided with steel and corrugated sheeting extensions at each end to form a 3T through-road DMU depot. Following the electrification of the line from Glasgow in 1986 it became redundant, and when the depot was taken over by Transrail in 1994 it was utilised as a wagon works. The site was subsequently transferred to EWS and then DB Schenker, and in 2010 was used for servicing shunters and visiting locomotives.

Building 2: A 2T through-road fuelling shed constructed in corrugated sheeting on a steel frame with a twin corrugated sheeting-clad lean-to-style roof was erected in the shed yard at NS34342277.

Building 3: After the depot closed to steam on 3 October 1966 the remaining portion of the steam shed was demolished in c1973 and a 1T dead-ended shed, constructed in brick and corrugated sheeting on steel frames with a single-pitched corrugated sheeting-clad roof was built on the site. This is located at NS34312275.

Operating company in 2010: DB Schenker
Allocation: Nil

Ayr depot on 21 July 2003 with unit No 156 430 passing on a northbound passenger working. This view, from the north west, shows Building 3 on the left and Building 1, the remnant of Ayr MPD, on the right. *Philip Stuart*

BEDFORD CAULDWELL

Cauldwell Walk, Bedford MK42 9DT

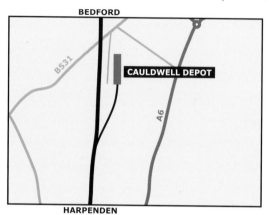

BEDFORD

CAULDWELL DEPOT

B531

A6

HARPENDEN

The yard is not visible from the line

Directions from Bedford St John's station: Turn right outside of the station along Ampthill Road and right into Victoria Road. Turn left at the end along Kempston Road, left into Cauldwell Walk and the depot is on the left.
(Distance approx 1.0 mile)

Originally a 4T dead-ended shed constructed in corrugated sheeting on a steel frame with a shallow Dutch barn-style roof, located at TL04444859 and opened by Southern on 11 September 2004 to service Class 319 units. The original purpose was to provide servicing facilities for these whilst the major work being undertaken at St Pancras station prevented them from accessing Selhurst depot.

After completion of the work the depot was retained and extended by one road on the west side in 2009.

Operating company in 2010: First Capital Connect

Allocation: Home base for Class 319 and 377/5 fleets

The south end of Cauldwell depot, viewed on 3 November 2004. The later IT extension was added on the left side of the building.
Chris Milner

BESCOT

Westmore Way, Wednesbury WS10 0UJ

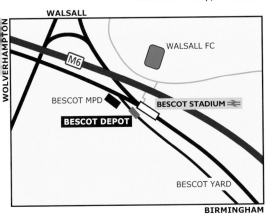

The yard is visible from the line

Directions from Bescot Stadium station:
Entrance to the shed is effected from the Walsall-bound platform.
(Distance approx 100yd)

A 3T through-road servicing shed, located at SP00629608 and opened by BR in May 1967. It was constructed in corrugated sheeting on a steel frame with a transverse multi-pitched roof and adjoined by a 1T through-road fuelling shed constructed in corrugated sheeting on a steel frame with a lean-to-style roof. It was built in the yard of the extant former steam shed and rapidly became the principal diesel depot for the area with an allocation of around 100 locomotives. By 1997 this had largely diminished and by 2010 the building was mainly being utilised as a wagon works.
Operating company in 2010: DB Schenker
Allocation: Nil (depot currently out of use for locomotive purposes)

Looking south east towards Bescot depot on 22 July 2008 with EWS Class 66 No 66 111 in the yard. *Nick Pigott*

11

BIRKENHEAD NORTH

Merseyside Electrics (2002) Ltd, Wallasey Bridge Road, Birkenhead CH41 1EB

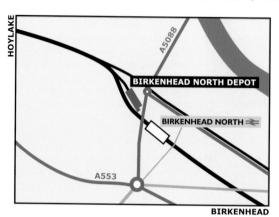

The yard is visible from the line

Directions from Birkenhead North station: Turn right outside of the station into Station Road, right into Wallasey Bridge Road and the depot is on the left, just past the railway bridge. (Distance approx 200yd)

A brick-built 3T dead-ended shed with a gable-style roof of corrugated sheeting, single-pitched with a high bay, located at SJ29679044 and utilised as the repair shop, adjoined by a brick built 4T dead-ended shed with a gable-style roof of corrugated sheeting, glazed and single-pitched, located at SJ29679041. It was opened by the London, Midland & Scottish Railway in 1938 and re-roofed in 2009.

Operating company in 2010: Merseyrail
Allocation: Home base for Class 507 and 508 fleets

The north west end of Birkenhead North depot on 27 June 1990. The incorrectly numbered DB977363/362 stands in front of the repair shed, whilst the servicing shed is on the right.

Philip Stuart

BIRMINGHAM SOHO

Vittoria Street, Warley B66 2NJ

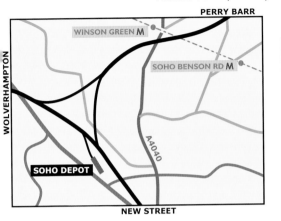

The yard is visible from the lines

**Directions from
Winson Green/Outer Circle
(Midland Metro) station**:
Turn right outside of the
station along Handsworth New
Road and right into Foundry
Road. At the end continue into
Vittoria Street and the depot
entrance is on the left.
(Distance approx 0.6 miles)

A 2T dead-ended shed, located at SP03938824 and constructed in corrugated sheeting and glazed panels on a steel frame with a gable-style single-pitched roof clad in corrugated sheeting. The depot, as an open-air stabling facility, had originally opened in the 1960s, and the building, although not officially opened by Central Trains until 16 April 1999, came into use on 15 January 1999.

Operating company in 2010: London Midland
Allocation: Home base for Class 323 fleet

Birmingham Soho depot on 10 April 2004 with the Birmingham Canal in the foreground. Class 08 depot shunter No 3973 (08 805) in LMS maroon livery can be seen stabled alongside of the building.
Philip Stuart

BIRMINGHAM TYSELEY

Warwick Road, Tyseley, Birmingham B11 2HJ

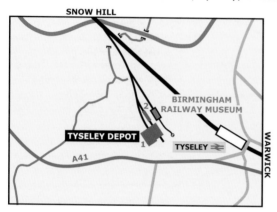

The yard is partially visible from the line

Directions from Tyseley station:
Turn right outside of the station and bear left along Warwick Road. The depot is on the right. (Distance approx 700yd)

Building 1: Originally a 7T dead-ended shed, located at SP10578407 and constructed in brick and corrugated sheeting on a steel frame with a transverse multi-pitched roof. It was opened by BR in 1961 and occupied the site of the former repair depot of Tyseley MPD. The building was extended to the north on 9 December 1965 with the addition of a 4T through-road shed constructed in corrugated sheeting with a corrugated sheeting-clad flat roof and again, prior to 1992, with a 1T through-road shed constructed in brick and corrugated sheeting on a steel frame with a glazed and corrugated sheeting-clad lean-to-style roof. In 1977 a 2T extension was added to the front end of the original building. This was constructed in corrugated sheeting on a steel frame with a glazed roof clad in corrugated sheeting, single-pitched and in gable style.

Building 2: A 1T through-road shed, located at SP10558413 and constructed in corrugated sheeting on a steel frame with a single-pitched roof of gable style and clad in corrugated sheeting. It was opened in c1992.

Operating companies in 2010: London Midland and Cross Country

Allocation: Home base for West Midlands DMUs

Birmingham Tyseley depot, viewed from the road entrance on 1 August 1993 and showing the 1965 4T and later 1T extensions. Birmingham Railway Museum can be seen on the right of the picture.

Philip Stuart

14

BOUNDS GREEN

Bridge Road, Wood Green, London N22 7SE

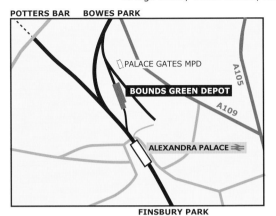

The yard is visible from both lines

Directions from Alexandra Palace station: Turn left outside the main entrance along Buckingham Road, right into Bridge Road and the depot is on the left. (Distance approx 200yd)

A 6T through-road shed with a 3T dead-ended repair shop adjoining the east side, located at TQ30159080 and constructed of brick and corrugated sheeting on steel frames, with a corrugated sheeting-clad and glazed roof in an unusual combination of lean-to and single-pitched styles. It was opened by BR in 1976 to service HSTs and was electrified in September 1987.

Operating company in 2010: East Coast
Allocation: Class 91 locomotives

The south end of Bounds Green depot on 18 September 1989. The ECML is in the foreground.
Philip Stuart

15

BOURNEMOUTH WEST

South West Trains, Nelson Road, Bournemouth BH4 9JA

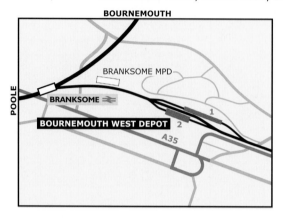

The depot and yard are not visible from the Branksome — Bournemouth line

Directions from Branksome station: Turn left outside of the station and then left along Poole Road. At the roundabout take the second exit, along Princess of Wales Road and then second left into Nelson Road. The depot is along this road on the left.
(Distance approx 1.1 miles)

Building 1: A 4T through-road shed located at SZ06699182 and constructed of brick with a corrugated sheeting-clad and glazed gable-style roof. It was built as a carriage shed by the Southern Railway in c1930 converted to an EMU depot by BR in 1967.

Building 2: Originally built as a 4T through-road shed, located at SZ06569182 and constructed in brick with a corrugated sheeting-clad steel frame and a corrugated sheeting and glazed gable-style roof. It was opened by BR in 1967 as the home base for 'REP' 'TC' stock, and a similarly constructed 2T extension was added at the western end in 1986 to accommodate the Class 442 sets that replaced them.

Building 2, the 1986 extension on the occasion of an EMU depot open day on 16 May1998.   *Philip Stuart*

The depot was downgraded upon the opening of Northam.

Operating company in 2010: South West Trains
Allocation: Nil

A general view of Bournemouth West depot on 2 January 1990. Building 1 is on the right with Building 2 on the left in the far distance.   *Philip Stuart*

BRIGHTON LOVERS WALK

Southern, New England Road, Brighton BN1 3TU

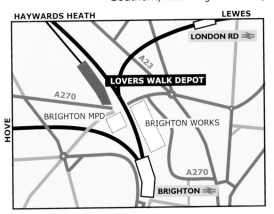

The yard is visible from the line

Directions from Brighton station: Turn right outside of the station into Terminus Road, bear right into Howard Place and continue along New England Road. The depot is on the left and entrance on the right.
(Distance approx 0.6 miles)

Located at TQ30740549 and opened by the LB&SCR in 1848 as a carriage works, it was converted to an EMU depot by the SR in 1933. At that time it was a brick-built 7T dead-ended shed with a transverse multi-pitched roof, and an additional 5T dead-ended shed, constructed in corrugated sheeting with a corrugated sheeting and glazed multi-pitched roof was built on the east side. A modernisation programme commenced in 2002, with the 5T building being reduced to 4T, and the depot was officially re-opened as a maintenance and servicing depot for Class 377 units on 11 December 2006.

Operating company in 2010: Southern

Allocation: Home base for part of the Class 377 fleet. Class 09 shunter No 09 026 (depot de-icer)

Brighton Lovers Walk depot during the 2002-2006 modernisation programme, on 20 March 2004. The difference in the styles of the two phases of building is clearly visible, with the earlier portion on the right.
Philip Stuart

BRISTOL BARTON HILL

Day's Road, Bristol BS5 0AJ

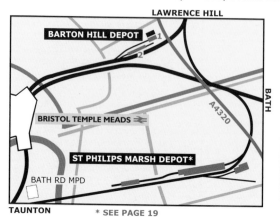

LAWRENCE HILL

BARTON HILL DEPOT

BATH

A4320

BRISTOL TEMPLE MEADS

ST PHILIPS MARSH DEPOT*

BATH RD MPD

TAUNTON   * SEE PAGE 19

The yard is visible from both of the lines

Directions from Bristol Temple Meads station: Turn right outside of the northwest exit and cross the harbour footbridge. Turn right along Avon Street, first left into Oxford Street and continue into Day's Road. The depot is on the right. (Distance approx 700yd)

Building 1: A stone-built 3TS dead-ended shed with a gable-style roof located at ST60477285. It was opened by the Midland Railway in c1855, closed in 1873 and then utilised solely as part of a wagon works until 23 July 1995 when a section of the building was adapted as a 1T diesel depot by RES.

Building 2: A steel-framed corrugated sheeting-clad 2T through-road shed with a gable-style roof, located at ST60397276 and opened by BR in 1960 to service the diesel Pullman sets. It closed in 1971 and became part of the wagon works but was refurbished and re-opened in 2002 by EWS.

In 2010 the depot was utilised for servicing visiting locomotives and 'Voyagers'.

Operating company in 2010: DB Schenker for XC

Allocation: Nil

The interesting collection of surviving shed buildings at Bristol Barton Hill depot on 28 August 2004. On the left is the former Bristol & Gloucester Railway 2TS shed dating back to 1850, in the middle is the ex-MR 3TS shed of c1855 which in 2010 was in use as the 1T diesel depot (Building 1) and on the right is the former GWR South Wales Junction 4TS shed of 1872.

Roger Griffiths

BRISTOL ST PHILIPS MARSH

Albert Road, Bristol BS2 0YG

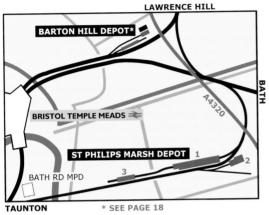

Passenger trains do not normally operate along this line

Directions from Bristol Temple Meads station:
Turn left along Temple Gate and continue along Bath Road. Turn left into Emery Road, cross the River Avon and turn right along Albert Road. At the roundabout take the second left along Albert Crescent and the depot is on the right.
(Distance approx 1.1 miles)

Building 1: A 3T through-road shed, located at ST60777216 and constructed of brick and corrugated sheeting on steel frames, with a corrugated sheeting-clad and glazed single gable-style roof. It was opened by BR in 1976 to service HSTs and extended at the east end in 1990. In 2002 a 1T through-road shed, constructed of corrugated sheeting on a steel frame with a lean-to-style corrugated sheeting-clad roof, was added on the south side.

Building 2: A 4T dead-ended shed, located at ST60977217 and constructed of brick and corrugated sheeting on steel frames, with a twin gable-style corrugated sheeting-clad and glazed pitched roof. It was opened by BR in 1959 as a DMU depot, known as Marsh Junction, and closed in 1970. It was then used as a permanent-way depot, and by 1991 it had been partitioned off, with permanent-way machines using the northern half and the southern portion utilised as an HST paint shop. In 2007 the southern half was extended at the west end and in 2010 accommodated 'Sprinters'.

Building 3: A 1T through-road shed, located at ST60397207 and constructed of corrugated sheeting on a steel frame with a corrugated sheeting-clad roof of single gable style.

Operating company in 2010: First Great Western
Allocation: Classes 143, 150, 153 and 158 units and HSTs

The 3T former HST shed, Building 1, viewed from the west at an open day at Bristol St Philips Marsh depot on 29 June 1991.   *Philip Stuart*

19

BURTON CENTRAL RIVERS

Bombardier Transportation Ltd, Barton-under-Needwood, Burton-upon-Trent DE13 8ES

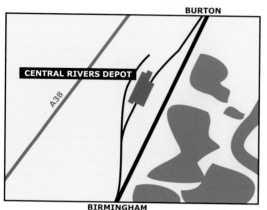

BURTON

CENTRAL RIVERS DEPOT

A38

BIRMINGHAM

The yard is partially visible from the line

Directions from Burton-upon-Trent station: Turn right outside of the station into Borough Road, continue along Station Street and turn right into Union Street. Continue along the B5018 and at the roundabout take the third exit along Orchard Street. Continue along the A5019 and St Peter's Bridge, cross the river and take the third exit at the roundabout into Main Street. Bear left into Rosliston Road, continue along Rosliston Road South and turn right into Walton Road. Continue along Main Street, turn right into Station Lane and proceed along Walton Lane and Station Road. Turn left at the roundabout, take the first exit at the next and the second at the next one. The depot is along this road.
(Distance approx 6.3 miles)

A 9T building with five through roads, located at SK20051755 and constructed in sheeting on steel frames with a triple shallow Dutch barn-style roof. Built on a greenfield site, it was officially opened on 18 September 2001 by Bombardier as a maintenance and servicing depot for Class 220 and 221 units.

Operating company in 2010: Bombardier for XC and Virgin West Coast.

Allocation: Home base for Class 220 and 221 fleets.

The north end of Central Rivers depot, viewed on 31 August 2002.   *Chris Milner*

CAMBRIDGE COLDHAMS LANE
Coldhams Road, Cambridge CB1 3EW

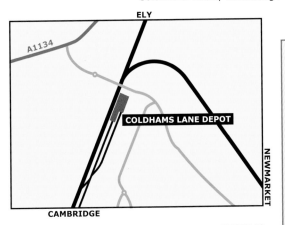

The yard is visible from the line

Directions from Cambridge station:
Go straight ahead along Station Road, turn first right into Tenison Road and second right along Devonshire Road. At the end turn right along Mill Road, cross the railway, turn left into Sedgewick Street and continue along Cromwell Road. Turn left at the end along Coldhams Lane, bear right into Coldhams Road and the depot is on the left.
(Distance approx 1.8 miles)

A 5T dead-ended shed, located at TL46795860 and constructed of brick and corrugated sheeting on steel frames, with a gable style of roof, glazed, clad in sheeting and twin-pitched. It was opened by BR in September 1958 as a DMU and shunter depot. The allocation was withdrawn from 18 January 1987 and it closed as an RES maintenance depot for parcels stock on 11 October 1996. The depot was re-opened by Central Trains in the week ending 22 February 1998 and in 2010 was used to service Class 170 units.
Operating company in 2010: Axiom Rail for XC
Allocation: Nil

Class 08 No 08 711 and Class 47 No 47 522 at the south end of Coldhams Lane depot on 14 September 1991.
Philip Stuart

21

CARDIFF CANTON

Arriva Trains Wales, Canton Diesel Depot, Leckwith Road, Cardiff CF11 8HP

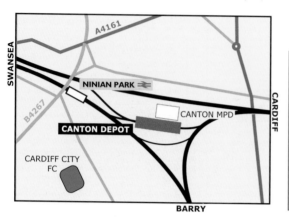

The yard is visible from the Barry line

Directions from Cardiff Central station:
Turn left into Central Square, then left into Wood Street and continue along Tudor Street and Ninian Park Road. Turn left at the end along Leckwith Road, cross the railway line and the depot entrance is on the left.
(Distance approx 1 mile)

A 10T through-road building, located at ST17107582 and constructed in brick with two 4T bays, one 2T bay and a triple-gable-style roof. It was opened by the GWR as a carriage shed in c1882 and converted into a DMU maintenance depot by BR following the closure of Cathays in November 1964.

Operating Company in 2010: Arriva Trains Wales

Allocation: Home base for Cardiff Valleys and Arriva Trains Wales fleets

The east end of Canton depot, viewed on 13 May 1992. The building on the right is the locomotive maintenance shed of the original Canton diesel depot that closed in January 2004. *Philip Stuart*

CARLISLE KINGMOOR

Direct Rail Services Limited, Kingmoor Depot, Etterby Road, Carlisle CA3 9NZ

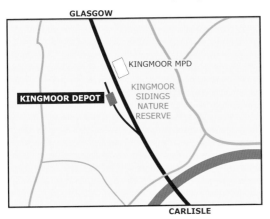

The yard is visible from the line

Directions from Carlisle Citadel station: Leave the station by the main entrance into Court Square, bear right along The Crescent and continue into Lowther Street. At the roundabout take the Bridgewater Road exit, cross the river and continue along Devonshire Terrace and Eden Mount. Turn left into Etterby Street, continue along Eden Place and Etterby Scaur and turn left into Etterby Road. The depot is past the railway bridge on the right. (Distance approx 2.5 miles)

A 4T through-road shed, located at NY38535752 and constructed in brick and corrugated sheeting on steel frames with a shallow-pitched corrugated sheeted and glazed roof. It was opened on 1 January 1968 by BR and closed in July 1988. The depot remained standing, unused and in a derelict condition, until 1999 when it was taken over by Direct Rail Services, stripped to the framework, re-clad in corrugated sheeting and re-opened as a DRS diesel depot in July of the same year.

Operating company in 2010: DRS
Allocation: Home base for DRS locomotive fleet

Kingmoor depot on 14 June 2003 with Nos 37 218 and 20 314 visible in the foreground.
Chris Milner

CARNFORTH

West Coast Railways, Jesson Way, Crag Bank, Carnforth LA5 9UR

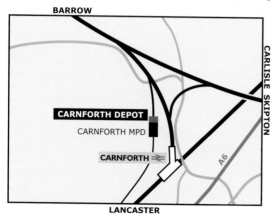

The yard is visible from the line

> **Directions from Carnforth station**:
> Turn left outside of the station along Wharton Road, continue under the railway bridge, turn left and pass under another railway bridge and the depot entrance is on the left-hand side.
> (Distance approx 800yd)

A 2T through-road shed, located at SD49597091 and constructed in concrete blocks and corrugated sheeting on steel frames with a shallow-pitched corrugated sheeted and glazed roof. Adjoined on the west side by a 3T through-road shed, located at SD49587091 and constructed in corrugated sheeting on steel frames with a shallow pitched corrugated sheeted and glazed roof. The two buildings were opened in 2007 and form an extension to the north end of the ex-BR steam shed which was built by the LMS in 1944.

Operating company in 2010: West Coast Railways
Allocation: Home base for the West Coast Railways locomotive fleet

Locomotives Nos 40 145, 33 029, 37 706, 55 022 and 47 798 line up on the occasion of the WCR/*Railway Magazine* Open Weekend at Carnforth depot on 26/27 July 2008.   *Nick Pigott*

CHESTER

Chester Train Care Depot, Hoole Bridge, Hoole Road, Chester CH2 3DJ

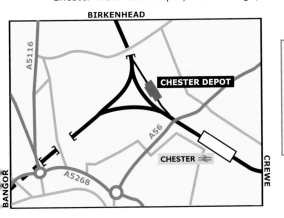

The yard is visible from the line

Directions from Chester station:
Turn right along Station Road, ascend the steps to Hoole Way, turn right and the depot is on the left, just past the railway bridge.
(Distance approx 200yd)

The site was originally occupied by Chester West MPD which closed to steam on 10 April 1960 and was converted to a DMU depot by BR in the same year. The depot was demolished in December 1998 and the site had to be totally cleared due to the excessive ground contamination caused by oil spillage and corrosive acids utilised by the washing plant. On 16 December 1999 the current 5T building with three through roads was formally opened by First North Western. It is located at SJ41006727 and constructed in brick and corrugated sheeting on steel frames with a shallow-pitched corrugated sheeted and glazed roof.

Operating company in 2010: Alstom
Allocation: Home base for Class 175 fleet

Chester depot, the north end viewed from a passing train on 19 July 2004.   *Philip Stuart*

CLACTON

Carnarvon Road, Clacton CO15 6QA

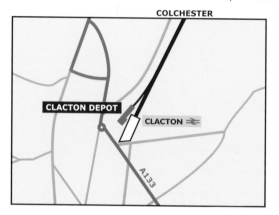

The yard is visible from the line

Directions from Clacton station:
Leave the station via the exit at Platform 4, turn right along Carnarvon Road and the depot entrance is on the right.
(Distance approx 50yd)

A 3T dead-ended shed, located at TM17601542 and constructed in brick and corrugated sheeting on a steel frame with a gable-style single-pitched roof. It was opened by BR on 17 July 1981 and the allocation was withdrawn in 1994. The building enjoyed numerous uses before it was scheduled to be re-opened in 2009 to accommodate Class 321/4s displaced by Class 350s on London Midland routes.

Operating company in 2010: National Express East Anglia
Allocation: Class 321 units

Clacton depot, closed and out of use on 11 October 2000. Although it was planned to re-open the building in 2009 this did not take place, and EMUs continued to stable in the shed yard.

Dave McGuire

CLAPHAM JUNCTION

South West Trains, Clapham Traincare Depot, 73-75 Plough Lane, London SW11 2UH

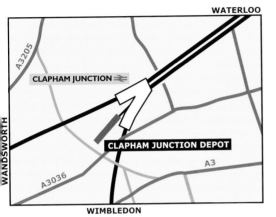

The yard is visible from the Wimbledon and Wandsworth lines

Directions from Clapham Junction station: Leave via the west exit, turn left along the approach road, left into Grant Road and left again into Plough Road. The depot is on the left.
(Distance approx 700yd)

A 5T dead-ended shed located at TQ27027540 and constructed in corrugated sheeting and glazed panels on a steel frame with a corrugated sheeting-clad and glazed gable -style single-pitched roof. It was originally built as a carriage shed by the L&SWR or SR and was utilised for EMUs from c1967. In 2010 it was used for servicing Classes 444, 450, 455 and 458 units.

Operating company in 2010: South West Trains
Allocation: Nil

Clapham Junction depot on 15 October 1992 with unit No 3157 in the yard.   *Philip Stuart*

COLCHESTER

Colchester North Station, Colchester CO1 1XD

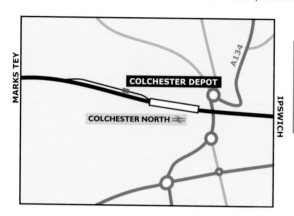

The yard is visible from the line

Directions from Colchester station:
Turn left outside of the north entrance to the station and a pathway leads to the depot. (Distance approx 300yd)

A 2T through-road shed constructed of brick and corrugated sheeting on steel frames, with a gable-style glazed roof of corrugated sheeting, located at TL98772648 and opened by BR in 1961. The allocation was withdrawn from 18 January 1987.
Operating company in 2010: National Express East Anglia
Allocation: 1 x Class 47 locomotive stabled for 'Thunderbird' duties

The east end of Colchester depot, viewed from the station on 26 June 2009 with Railfreight Class 90 No 90 046 running through on the freight lines.
Nick Pigott

CREWE ELECTRIC
Wistaston Road, Crewe CW2 7RL

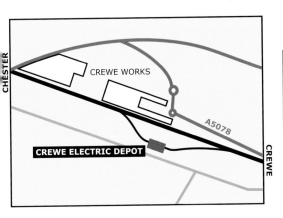

The yard is not visible from the line

Directions from Crewe station:
Turn left along Nantwich Road, right into Mill Street and turn left at the roundabout along Oak Street. Continue into Wistaston Road and the depot is on the right, opposite the end of Stewart Street.
(Distance approx 1.3 miles)

A 4T through-road shed constructed of brick and corrugated sheeting on steel frames, with a single gable-style glazed and pitched roof clad in corrugated sheeting. It is located at SJ69435568 and was opened by BR in 1959 in preparation for the commencement of the 25kV ac Manchester—Crewe services on 12 September 1960. As well as maintenance and servicing the depot is also utilised for locomotive storage.

Operating company in 2010: DB Schenker
Allocation: Home base for Class 92 locomotives and Class 325 fleet

The east end of Crewe Electric depot, viewed on 17 June 1999.   *Dave McGuire*

CREWE GRESTY BRIDGE

Direct Rail Services Ltd, Gresty Bridge Depot, Gresty Road, Crewe CW2 5AA

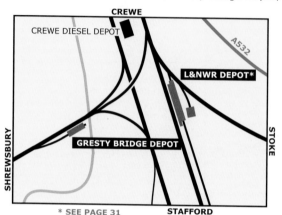

* SEE PAGE 31

The yard is partially visible from the line

Directions from Crewe station:
Turn left along Nantwich Road and left into Gresty Road. The depot is on the right, just after the railway bridge.
(Distance approx 1.2 miles)

Located at SJ70905374 and opened by the GWR in c1905 as a 2T wagon works, it was built in brick with a slated gable-style roof. The building was taken over by Direct Rail Services in 2007, totally refurbished with a new roof clad in corrugated sheeting, and re-opened on 23 March 2007 as a 2T diesel depot. In 2010 it was utilised for servicing Class 20, 37, 47 and 66 locomotives.

Operating company in 2010: DRS
Allocation: Nil

Above: An interior view of Crewe Gresty Road depot on 19 July 2009 with Nos 20 313, 20 310 and 66 411 inside the shed.

Below: On the same day Class 47 No 47 832 *Solway Princess* was in the yard.
Richard Gennis

CREWE L&NWR

L&NWR, Crewe Carriage Shed, Weston Road, Crewe CW1 6NE

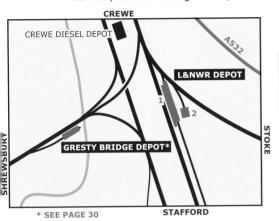

The yard is visible from both of the lines

Directions from Crewe station:
Turn right along Nantwich Road and right at the roundabout into Weston Road. After about 0.8 miles turn right into a private road and this leads to the depot.
(Distance approx 1.1 miles)

Building 1: A 7T through-road brick-built carriage shed with twin gable-style pitched roofs located at SJ71465386 and opened by the LNWR before 1910. It was utilised by BR in the 1960s as a stabling point for DMUs and EMUs, and the 3T bay on the west side was refurbished at some point after 1996 with a corrugated sheeting-clad and glazed pitched roof.

Building 2: A 3T through-road shed constructed of concrete blocks and corrugated sheeting on steel frames, with a single gable-style corrugated sheeting-clad and glazed pitched roof adjoined by a similarly constructed 1T through-road shed. It was built by L&NWR in 1999 and is located at SJ71535383.

The depot is utilised to maintain and service 'Voyagers', 'Desiros', 'Sprinters', Freightliner's Class 66, 86 and 90 locomotives and locomotive-hauled stock.

Operating company in 2010: Arriva
Allocation: Nil

Building 1 at Crewe L&NWR depot on 23 July 1993. Viewed from the north end, with the WCML on the right, this shows the building some years before it was refurbished. *Philip Stuart*

31

CROFTON

Crofton Permanent Way Depot, Doncaster Road, Crofton, Wakefield WF4 1RS

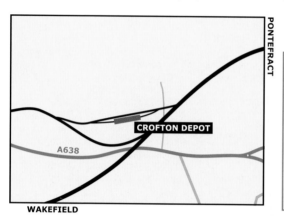

The yard is partially visible from the line

Directions from Wakefield Kirkgate station: Turn left into Station Passage and left along Doncaster Road. Follow this road for about 2.4 miles and, just after a railway overbridge and nearly opposite to Lodge Lane, turn left into a lane. The depot is along here on the left.
(Distance approx 2.5 miles)

A 2T through-road shed, located at SE36811905 and constructed in corrugated sheeting on a steel frame with a corrugated sheeting-clad twin-pitched roof of gable style. It was opened on 27 February 2001 by Bombardier as an outstation of Horbury Works as a temporary base for commissioning 'Voyager' units. In 2006 it was upgraded to a maintenance depot and in 2010 was servicing Class 170/3 units.
Operating company in 2010: Bombardier
Allocation: Nil

Constructed on the site of a former permanent-way yard, Crofton depot is viewed from the east on 17 August 2001,
Philip Stuart

DERBY ETCHES PARK

Deadmans Lane, Derby DE24 8BS

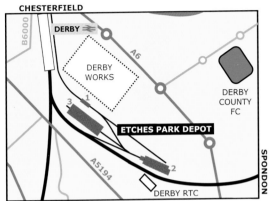

The yard is visible from the line

Directions from Derby station:
At the main entrance turn left along Midland Road and left into London Road. Turn left into Deadmans Lane and the depot is on the left.
(Distance approx 1.2 miles)

Building 1: A 2T through-road shed built on part of the site of Derby MPD and constructed in corrugated sheeting on a steel frame with a corrugated sheeting-clad transverse multi-pitched roof. It is located at SK36433523 and was opened by BR in 1964 as a locomotive depot. In 2010 it was employed as a fuelling shed.

Building 2: A purpose-built 5T dead-ended shed constructed in brick and corrugated sheeting on steel frames, with a twin-pitched gable-style glazed roof clad in corrugated sheeting, located at SK36823489 and opened by BR in 1959 initially as a DMU and carriage shed. In 2010 it was a DMU and HST depot, servicing Class 170 sets.

Building 3: A 3T through-road shed, located at SK36433513 and constructed in steel sheeting on a steel frame with a corrugated sheeting-clad and glazed single-pitch roof of gable style. It was constructed in 2009, and during the excavations three turntable pits and 23 ashpit roads were uncovered.

Operating company in 2010: East Midlands Trains

Allocation: Home base for Class 222 fleet

Looking south east at Building 2 at Derby Etches Park depot on 9 July 1992.   *Philip Stuart*

DIDCOT MILTON PARK

Didcot Parkway Station, Didcot OX11 7NR

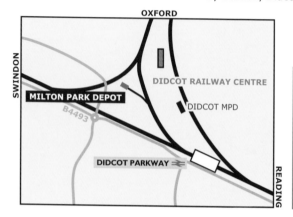

The yard is visible from the Oxford line and partially visible from the Swindon line

Directions from Didcot Parkway station: Turn right outside of the station and cross the footbridge on the right into the car park. The depot is at the end of a drive leading from the right-hand side of the car park.
(Distance approx 200yd)

A 1T dead-ended shed constructed in brick and corrugated sheeting on steel frames with a corrugated sheeting-clad single-pitched roof of gable style, located at SU52109091 and opened in 1994 by Trainload Freight SouthEast to service and carry out minor repairs and exams on its locomotives based in the area.

Operating company in 2010: DB Schenker
Allocation: Nil

Milton Park depot on 13 April 1999 with Class 37 No 37 802 in the yard.   *Dave McGuire*

DOLLANDS MOOR

Bargrove, Newington, Folkestone CT18 8BH

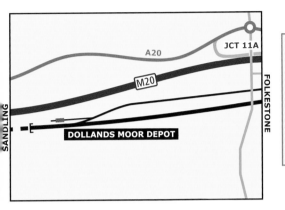

The yard is visible from the line

Directions from Sandling station:
Turn right outside of the station into Sandling Road and right along Ashford Road. Turn left at the roundabout, cross over the M20 and the depot entrance is on the left.
(Distance approx 2.8 miles)

A 1T through-road shed constructed in corrugated sheeting on a steel frame with a corrugated sheeting-clad roof of Dutch barn style, located at TR16323697 and opened in 1994 to service the Channel Tunnel freight stock.
Operating company in 2010: DB Schenker
Allocation: Nil

Looking east towards Dollands Moor depot on 24 June 1995   *Philip Stuart*

DONCASTER CARR
Ten Pound Walk, Doncaster DN4 5HX

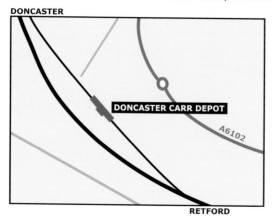

DONCASTER

RETFORD

The yard is partially visible from the line

Directions from Doncaster station:
Turn right along the station approach road, continue into West Street and turn right into St Sepulchre Gate West. Turn right along Cleveland Street and, at the interchange, turn left into Kelham Street. The depot entrance is at the end of a cul-de-sac on the right.
(Distance approx 0.7 miles)

A brick-built 9T through-road shed with a four-pitched corrugated sheeting-clad roof, located at SE57610167 and opened by the GNR on 25 March 1876. Doncaster MPD closed to steam in May 1966 and was reduced to a 6T structure, utilising the 2T dead-ended repair shop and an adjoining 4T through-road portion of the running shed. The remainder of the building was demolished between 1981 and 1983, and by 2009 part of the depot was in use as a wagon works.
Operating company in 2010: DB Schenker
Allocation: Nil

Doncaster Carr depot on 16 June 2009.

Nick Pigott

EAST HAM

Stevenage Road, East Ham, London E6 2AU

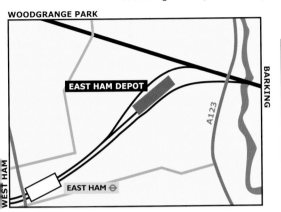

WOODGRANGE PARK

EAST HAM DEPOT

BARKING

A123

WEST HAM

EAST HAM ⊖

The yard is visible from the line

**Directions from
East Ham (LT) station**:
Turn left along High Street
North, left into Burges Road
and left along Southend Road.
Turn left into Stevenage Road
and the depot is on the left.
(Distance approx 0.7 miles)

An 11T dead-ended shed constructed in corrugated sheeting and glazed panels on a steel frame with a corrugated sheeting-clad and glazed flat roof. It is located at TQ43108471 and was opened by BR in 1961, re-roofed in 1984 and re-roofed again in 1999.
Operating company in 2010: C2C
Allocation: Home base for Class 357 fleet

East Ham depot viewed from an up train on 29 July 1989.   *Philip Stuart*

37

EASTLEIGH

DB Schenker, Campbell Road, Eastleigh SO50 5AE

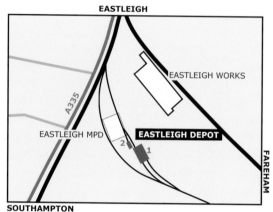

EASTLEIGH

EASTLEIGH WORKS

A335

EASTLEIGH MPD

EASTLEIGH DEPOT

FAREHAM

SOUTHAMPTON

The yard is partially visible from the line

Directions from Eastleigh station:
Turn left outside of the station into Southampton Road, turn left along Campbell Road and the depot is on the right.
(Distance approx 0.5 miles)

The depot was opened by BR in 1958 and constructed in the shed yard at the south end of Eastleigh MPD. The steam shed was closed by BR on 9 July 1967 and subsequently demolished.

Building 1: Located at SU45831795 and originally built as a 4T dead-ended shed, it is constructed in brick and glazed panels on a steel frame with a single-pitched gable-style glazed roof clad in corrugated sheeting. In 1965 it was lengthened at the south end and a 4T through-road extension was also added on the west side. The extension is located at SU45791795 and constructed in brick and glazed panels on a steel frame with a twin-pitched gable-style glazed roof clad in corrugated sheeting.

Building 2: A 1T through-road fuelling shed located at SU45751798 and constructed in corrugated sheeting on a steel frame with a corrugated sheeting-clad single-pitched roof of gable style. It was opened in 1998.

Operating company in 2010: DB Schenker
Allocation: Nil

The 1T fuelling shed, Building 2, at Eastleigh depot on 8 May 2001. The western extension to Building 1 can be seen on the left of the picture.   *Philip Stuart*

EAST WIMBLEDON

South West Trains, Wimbledon Traincare Depot, Durnsford Road, London SW19 8EG

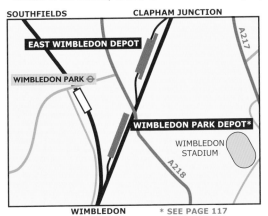

SOUTHFIELDS   CLAPHAM JUNCTION

EAST WIMBLEDON DEPOT

WIMBLEDON PARK ⊖

WIMBLEDON PARK DEPOT*

WIMBLEDON STADIUM

A217

A218

WIMBLEDON   * SEE PAGE 117

The yard is visible from the line

Directions from Wimbledon Park (LT) station:
Turn right outside of the station into Arthur Road, turn right again into Durnsford Road and the depot is on the left.
(Distance approx 500yd)

A 7T through-road shed located at TQ25627230 and constructed of brick and corrugated sheeting on steel frames with a twin gable-style corrugated sheeting-clad and glazed pitched roof. It was built on part of the site occupied by the Durnsford Road EMU depot and power station complex that had been opened by the L&SWR in 1915. The power station supplied the electrified lines until the early 1960s when electricity was drawn from the National Grid, and it became redundant whilst the EMU shed was closed in 1973. The site was cleared in 1974 and the depot opened on 3 October 1974.

Operating company in 2010: South West Trains
Allocation: Home base for Class 455 and 458 fleets

East Wimbledon depot, viewed from Durnsford Road bridge on 8 June 2009. The former Durnsford Road EMU depot, which closed in 1973, was sited on the left.   *Philip Stuart*

EDINBURGH CRAIGENTINNY
Mountcastle Crescent, Edinburgh EH8 7TE

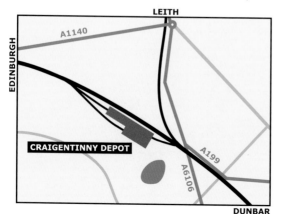

The yard is visible from the line

Directions from Brunstane station:
Turn left outside of the station and take the second exit at the roundabout, along The Jewel. Turn right at the end along Duddingston Park, continue into Baileyfield Road and the depot is on the left, just before the railway bridge.
(Distance approx 1.6 miles)

An 8T depot constructed in brick and corrugated sheeting on a steel frame with corrugated sheeting-clad single-pitch roofs of gable style and consisting of a 1T through-road fuelling shed, a 1T through-road shed and repair shop, a 2T through-road shed and a 4T dead-ended shed. It was opened by BR in 1977, electrified in 1991 and is located at NT29857387. It was built to service HSTs, and in 2010 was also employed for servicing and maintaining Class 91s and Mk 4 stock as well as servicing and fuelling Class 220 and 221 units for Arriva CrossCountry.
Operating company in 2010: East Coast
Allocation: Home base for East Coast HST fleet and 2 x Class 08 shunters (depot pilots)

The east end of Craigentinny depot, viewed on 11 July 2003.   *Chris Milner*

EDINBURGH HAYMARKET

Russell Road, Edinburgh EH12 5NB

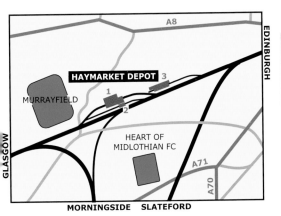

The yard is visible from the line

Directions from Haymarket station:
Turn left outside of the station into Haymarket Terrace and continue along West Coates. Turn left into Roseburn Street, left into Russell Road and the depot is on the right.
(Distance approx 0.8 miles)

Originally the site of the 8T through-road Haymarket MPD which was opened by the North British Railway in 1894 and closed to steam by BR on 9 September 1963. The 2T repair shop was retained whilst the remainder was demolished and progressively replaced with purpose-built structures.

Building 1: A 2T dead-ended shed, located at NT22917284 and constructed in brick with a glazed and corrugated sheeting-clad single-pitch roof of gable style. It was converted from the steam repair shop by BR in 1963 and enlarged on the south side in 1966 with a 3T through-road shed constructed in brick with a corrugated sheeting-clad and glazed northlight-pattern roof and a 3T through-road shed constructed in brick and corrugated sheeting on a steel frame with a corrugated sheeting-clad roof similar in style to that of the steam repair shop.

In 1977 a brick-built 1T extension with a gable-style roof was added at the western end and in c1988 a corrugated sheeting-clad steel-framed 1T lean-to shed was built on the south side.

Building 2: A 2T through-road shed, located at NT22987280 and constructed in brick and corrugated sheeting on a steel frame with a twin corrugated sheeting-clad single gable-style roof. It was opened in c1987 and extended at the west end in c1990.

Building 3: A 3T through-road shed, located at NT23167288 and constructed in corrugated sheeting on a steel frame with a roof the same as that of Building 2. It was opened on 13 February 2007.

The depot was originally built to house locomotives, but following the closure of Leith Central in 1972 it gradually became a DMU facility.

Operating company in 2010: First Scotrail

Allocation: Home base for most Scottish DMUs

Edinburgh Haymarket depot on 15 August 1989. At this time it was being rebuilt as a 'Sprinter' depot and Building 1, with the yellow and black doors, can be seen in the centre with Building 2 on the extreme right.
Philip Stuart

EDINBURGH MILLERHILL

Millerhill Freight Complex, Whitehill Road, Musselburgh EH21 8RZ

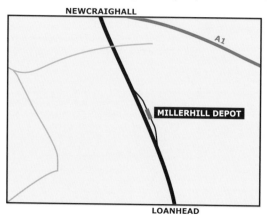

Passenger trains do not normally operate along this line

Directions from Newcraighall station:
Turn right outside of the station along a footpath and continue under the A1.
Turn right into Whitehill Road and the depot entrance is on the left.
(Distance approx 0.7 miles)

A 1T through-road shed, located at NT32307095 and constructed in brick and glazed sheeting on a steel frame with a flat corrugated sheeted roof. It was opened by BR in 1962 and in 2010 was in use for the servicing of shunters and visiting locomotives.
Operating company in 2010: DB Schenker
Allocation: Nil

Edinburgh Millerhill depot, with Class 66 No 66 098 alongside, on 25 July 2003. *Philip Stuart*

EXETER

St Davids Station, Exeter EX4 4NT

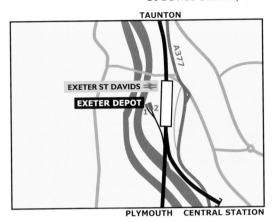

The yard is visible from the line

Directions from Exeter St Davids station:
Turn left outside of the station and follow the path to Cowley Bridge Road. Bear left into Station Road, cross the railway and the depot is on the left.
(Distance approx 300yd)

PLYMOUTH   CENTRAL STATION

The depot has been constructed within the original brick walls of Exeter MPD which was opened by the Bristol & Exeter Railway in 1864 and closed to steam by BR on 14 October 1963. At this point the building was roofless and locomotives stabled in the shed roads until 1979 when the 1T depot (Building 1) opened in the westernmost portion. In 1987 a lightweight roof was erected over the two eastern tracks and this was removed in 1994 to accommodate the construction of the 2T depot (Building 2).

Building 1: A 1T dead-ended shed, located at SX91059338 and constructed in brick and corrugated sheeting on steel frames with a corrugated sheeting-clad single-pitched roof of gable style.

Building 2: A 2T dead-ended shed, located at SX91069339 and constructed in brick and corrugated sheeting on a steel frame. The roof is exactly the same as that of Building 1, except for the addition of glazing. The building utilised the east wall of the former steam shed and was opened by Arriva Wales & West in 1994.

Operating company in 2010: First Great Western

Allocation: Home base for West of England DMUs

Exeter depot on 18 July 1997. The walls of the former Exeter MPD shed can clearly be seen with the 1T Building 1 on the left and the later 2T Building 2 on the right, housing unit No 150 251.

Philip Stuart

FARNHAM

Wrecclesham Road, Farnham GU9 8TY

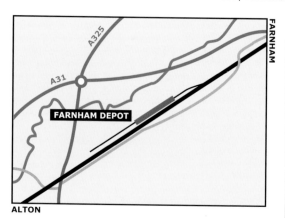

The yard is visible from the line

Directions from Farnham station:
Bear right across the station yard and left down Station Hill. Turn left along the by-pass and second left into Weydon Lane. Cross over the railway and continue to the end, passing the depot on the right. Turn right into Wrecclesham Road, pass under the railway and the depot entrance is on the right.
(Distance approx 1.0 mile)

The depot was originally built by the Southern Railway in 1936 as a 5T dead-ended shed constructed of brick with a corrugated sheeted and glazed single-pitch gable-style roof. Located at SU83204577, it was subsequently modified when two of the roads were extended through the rear of the depot, and in 2010 was used for servicing Class 450 units.

Operating company in 2010: South West Trains
Allocation: Nil

Farnham depot on 18 May 1991 with unit No 3519 occupying road No 2.　　　*Philip Stuart*

FORT WILLIAM TOM-NA-FAIRE

Tom-na-Faire Depot, North Road, Fort William PH33 6PP

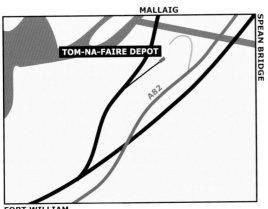

The yard is visible from the Mallaig line

Directions from Fort William station:
Turn left outside of the station into Belford Road and continue along North Road. A road leads to the depot from the left-hand side.
(Distance approx 1.5 miles)

A 1T dead-ended shed, located at NN11977521 and constructed in brick and corrugated sheeting on a steel frame with a gable-style pitched corrugated-sheeted roof. It was opened by BR in 1975 and, as well as servicing visiting diesel locomotives, steam locomotives are based here during the summer season.
Operating company in 2010: DB Schenker
Allocation: Nil

Tom-na-Faire depot on 4 August 1994. This view looking north east shows the diesel shed, with Class 37 Nos 37 153 and 37 404 stabled outside of the depot entrance. *Philip Stuart*

45

FRATTON

Goldsmith Avenue, Southsea PO4 0AT

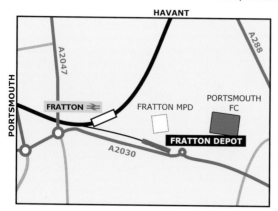

The yard is partially visible from the line

Directions from Fratton station:
Turn left outside of the station, cross the footbridge and turn left along Goldsmith Avenue. The depot is on the left.
(Distance Approx 600yd)

A 4T dead-ended shed, located at SZ65689990 and constructed in brick with a corrugated sheeted and glazed gable-style single-pitched roof. It was opened in 1937 by the Southern Railway and although the allocation was withdrawn in 1990 the depot officially re-opened on 30 November 1994. In 2010 it was used to service Class 444 and 450 units.
Operating company in 2010: South West Trains
Allocation: Nil

Fratton depot viewed from Fratton station on 6 April 2000.

Dave McGuire

GILLINGHAM

Gillingham Road, Gillingham ME7 4QU

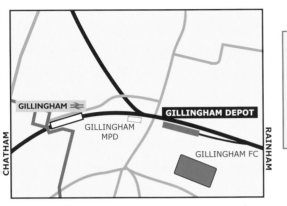

The yard is visible from the line

Directions from Gillingham station:
Turn left outside of the station yard along Balmoral Road and left at the end along Gillingham Road. The depot is on the right.
(Distance approx 0.5 miles)

A 4T dead-ended shed, located at TQ78226837 and constructed in brick and corrugated sheeting on steel frames with a corrugated sheeting-clad gable-style single-pitched roof. It was opened in 1939 by the Southern Railway and in 2010 was being used to service Class 465 and 466 units.
Operating company in 2010: South Eastern
Allocation: Nil

The east end of Gillingham depot on 16 September 1989.

Philip Stuart

GLASGOW CORKERHILL

First Scotrail Ltd, Corkerhill Depot, Corkerhill Place, Glasgow G52 1RU

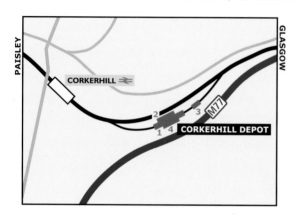

The yard is visible from the line

Directions from Corkerhill station:
Turn left into Corkerhill Road, left into Corkerhill Place and the depot is on the left.
(Distance approx 800yd)

Originally the site of the 6TS through-road Corkerhill MPD which was opened by the Glasgow & South Western Railway in 1896 and closed to steam by BR on 1 May 1967. It became a DMU depot when one of the three 2T bays was retained for diesel use and over the years between 1973 and 1978 the steam shed was progressively demolished and replaced with purpose-built structures:

Building 1: A 4T through-road shed, located at NS54556276 and constructed in brick and corrugated sheeting on a steel frame with a corrugated sheeting-clad single-pitched roof. It was built on the site of the former steam shed and opened in c1973-78, becoming an EMU shed in 1986.

Building 2: A 1T through-road shed, located at NS54536278 and constructed in brick and corrugated sheeting on a steel frame with a roof as on Building 1. It was built on the site of the former steam shed repair depot and incorporates a high bay section.

Building 3: A 2T through-road fuelling shed, located at NS54746288 and constructed in corrugated sheeting on a steel frame with a shallow-pitched corrugated sheeting-clad roof.

Building 4: A 2T dead-ended shed constructed in corrugated sheeting on a steel frame with a roof as on Building 3, located at NS54556275 and opened in March 1994 by Strathclyde for DMUs.

Operating company in 2010: Strathclyde

Allocation: Home base for DMUs operating on South of Clyde services.

The west end of Corkerhill depot, viewed on 19 November 2008. *Peter Woods*

48

GLASGOW EASTFIELD

Carron Crescent, Springburn, Glasgow G22 6BY

The yard is visible from the line

Directions from Ashfield station:
Turn left along Ashfield Street, left into Hawthorn Street and, after the railway bridge, left into Carron Crescent.
The depot is at the end of this road.
(Distance approx 0.7 miles)

Originally the site of Glasgow Eastfield MPD which was opened by the NBR in September 1904 and closed to steam by BR in November 1966. The shed was progressively demolished in 1969 and a large 13T depot built in its place. This closed on 21 August 1992 with demolition following in 1995, and by 2005 it had been replaced with stabling sidings.

In c1980 a 1T through-road fuelling shed was built in the shed yard by BR. It was constructed in corrugated sheeting with a corrugated sheeting-clad single-pitched roof and was located at NS60006876. This was subsequently closed and replaced on the same site by a 2T DMU servicing shed which was opened by Scotrail on 12 December 2004. It is constructed in corrugated sheeting and glazed panels on a steel frame with a corrugated sheeting-clad and glazed single-pitched and gabled roof.

Operating company in 2010: First Scotrail
Allocation: Nil

Once the site of massive steam and diesel depots, all that remained here on 4 July 2006 was the 2T Eastfield depot which was opened in 2004. *Philip Stuart*

49

GLASGOW POLMADIE

Alstom, Glasgow Traincare Centre, 109 Polmadie Road, Glasgow G5 0BA

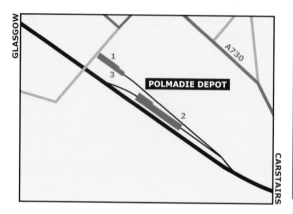

POLMADIE DEPOT

The yard is visible from the line

Directions from Bridgeton station:
Turn left outside of the station into Main Street, continue along Shawfield Drive, cross the bridge and turn right into Rutherglen Road. Turn left into Polmadie Road and the depot is on the left, just before the railway bridge.
(Distance approx 1.4 miles)

Originally the site of Polmadie MPD, a 14TS shed that was rebuilt by the LMS in 1925 and closed to steam by BR on 1 May 1967. The shed was used as a diesel depot until c1975 when it was demolished and only the 2T repair shop on the north side of the building was retained.

Building 1: A brick-built 2T dead-ended shed with a high-bay single-pitched roof located at NS59836267 and originally built as a steam repair depot. It was converted to diesel use by BR in 1963.

Building 2: A 5T through-road shed, located at NS60106242 and constructed in brick and corrugated sheeting on steel frames with a single-pitched corrugated sheet clad roof. It was opened

This view, taken on 27 July 1994 shows the 2T shed opened in 1985 (Building 3) with the high bay former steam shed repair depot (Building 1) to the rear.
Philip Stuart

by BR in c1978 as a carriage shed for APT use and extended at the east end in 1994 for EPNS.

Building 3: A 2T dead-ended shed constructed in brick and corrugated sheeting on steel frames with a single-pitched roof of corrugated sheeting, located at NS59876264 and opened in 1985.

In 2010 the depot was in use for the servicing and maintenance of Class 390 units.

Operating company in 2010: Alstom for Virgin West Coast

Allocation: Nil

Building 2 at Glasgow Polmadie depot on 5 August 2003.
Philip Stuart

50

GLASGOW SHIELDS

St Andrew's Drive, Glasgow G41 5SG

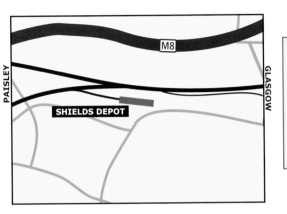

The yard is visible from the line

Directions from Shields Road (SPT Subway) station: Turn right outside of the station along Scotland Street, left into Shields Road and right into St Andrew's Drive. The depot is on the right.
(Distance approx 0.6 miles)

A 4T shed with one through road, located at NS56956394 and constructed in brick and corrugated sheeting on a steel frame with a corrugated sheeting-clad and glazed gabled single-pitched roof. It was opened by BR in 1966 and later extended at the east end. A further extension was planned to come into use in 2010.

Operating company in 2010: First Scotrail Strathclyde
Allocation: Home base for all Scottish EMUs

Shields depot on 19 November 2008.

Nick Pigott

GROVE PARK

Baring Road, London SE12 0DZ

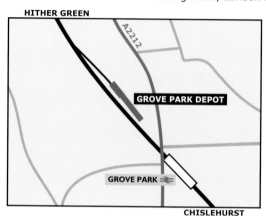

The yard is visible from the line

**Directions from
Grove Park station:**
Turn right outside of the
station along Baring Road and
the depot is on the left.
(Distance approx 100yd)

A 6T dead-ended shed, located at TQ40437245 and constructed in brick and corrugated sheeting with a corrugated sheeting-clad and glazed single-pitch gabled roof. It was opened by BR in 1962 and in 2010 was being used to service Class 465 and 466 units.
Operating company in 2010: South Eastern
Allocation: Nil

Grove Park depot receiving attention to the roof and gable end on 20 June 1998.   *Philip Stuart*

HITHER GREEN

Manor Lane, Hither Green, London SE12 0UA

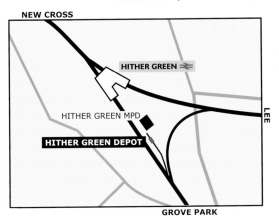

The yard is visible from the Grove Park line

Directions from Hither Green station: A path leads to the depot from the south end of Platform 4. (Distance approx 200yd)

A 2T through-road shed, located at TQ39247413 and constructed in corrugated sheeting, with a gabled corrugated sheeting-clad single-pitch roof incorporating a raised section at the north end. It opened in 1997 to replace a similar 2T structure that opened in c1970 and is built in the yard of the former steam shed.

Operating company in 2010: DB Schenker
Allocation: Nil

Hither Green depot viewed from the south on 20 June 1998. The high-bay section is clearly visible at the north end of the building and beyond that is the northlight-pattern roof of the still-extant Hither Green MPD.
Philip Stuart

HOLYHEAD

Arriva Trains Wales, Light Maintenance Depot, London Road, Holyhead LL65 2PB

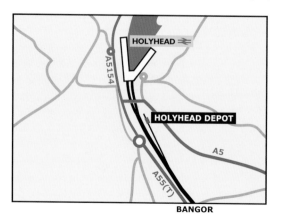

The yard is visible from the line

Directions from Holyhead station:
At the end of the main drive, turn left along London Road. A short cul-de-sac, on the right-hand side and nearly opposite Wian Street, leads to the depot.
(Distance approx 400yd)

A 1T through-road shed, located at SH24888195 and constructed in corrugated sheeting on a steel frame with a corrugated sheeting-clad gabled single-pitched roof. It was built in the yard of the former Holyhead MPD and opened by BR in 1989. In 2010 it was used to service visiting locomotives and DMUs.

Operating company in 2010: Arriva Trains Wales
Allocation: Nil

The north end of Holyhead depot, viewed on 28 March 1995.   *Dave McGuire*

HORNSEY

Hampden Road, Hornsey, London N8 0HF

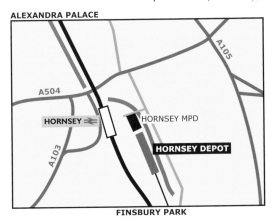

The yard is visible from the line

Directions from Hornsey station:
Access to the depot is gained from the east end of the station footbridge.
(Distance approx 200yd)

A 6T dead-ended shed, located at TQ31108905 and constructed in corrugated sheeting on a steel frame with a corrugated sheeting-clad flat roof. It was built in the shed yard of the former Hornsey MPD and opened by BR in 1976.

Operating company in 2010: First Capital Connect

Allocation: Home base for Class 313, 317 and 365 fleets

The south end of Hornsey depot viewed on 31 March 1991.   *Philip Stuart*

55

HULL BOTANIC GARDENS
Kimberley Street, Kingston-upon-Hull HU3 1HH

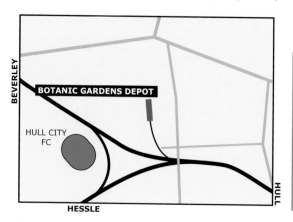

The yard is not visible from the line

**Directions from
Hull Paragon station:**
Turn left through the bus station, cross the car park and turn right into Park Street. Turn left along Londesbrough Street, right into Argyle Street and left into Kimberley Street. The depot is at the end of this cul-de-sac.
(Distance approx 0.8 miles)

Located at TA08142924 and originally opened by the NER in 1901 as a 2RH brick-built shed, it was rebuilt by BR as a 5TS through-road depot with a concrete and glass roof, and closed to steam on 14 June 1959. It was then utilized as a DMU and shunter depot but the allocation was withdrawn from 18 January 1987 and it was downgraded to a fuelling point. By 1991 it had been partially demolished and reduced to a 2T structure but was re-roofed and refurbished in 2009 and used in 2010 to service visiting DMUs.
Operating company in 2010: Northern
Allocation: Nil

The 2T remains of Hull Botanic Gardens depot on 7 August 1991 with units Nos 156 484 and 142 075 on view.
Philip Stuart

ILFORD

Bombardier Transportation (UK) Ltd, Ley Street, Ilford IG1 4BP

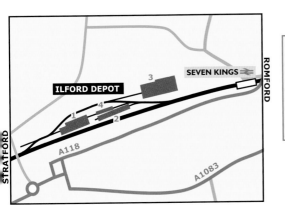

The yard is visible from the line

**Directions from
Seven Kings station**:
Turn left along Cameron Road,
left again into Aldeborough
Road and the depot is on the
right.
(Distance approx 600yd)

Building 1: A 6T shed with four through roads, located at TQ44478688 and constructed in brick and corrugated sheeting on a steel frame with a glazed and corrugated sheeting-clad gabled high-pitched roof over each bay. Known as 'A Shop' it was opened by BR in 1949 as a DC EMU shed and converted to AC on 21 November 1960.

Building 2: A 3T dead-ended shed located at TQ44678695 and built in brick with a gable-style corrugated sheeting-clad and glazed pitched roof. Known as 'B Shop' it was opened by BR in 1949 as a DC EMU shed and converted to AC on 21 November 1960.

Building 3: Originally a 16T dead-ended shed, located at TQ44938707 and constructed in corrugated sheeting on a steel frame with a steel and glazed flat roof. It was opened as an AC EMU shed by BR on 21 November 1960, re-roofed in 1984 and re-roofed again, with four shallow pitches, by 2000.

Building 4: A 1T through-road shed, located at TQ44658697 and constructed in corrugated sheeting on a steel frame with a glazed and corrugated sheeting-clad gabled single-pitched roof. It was opened in c2000.

Current operating companies: Buildings 1, 2 and 4: Bombardier, Building 3: NXEA

Allocation: Home base for Class 315, 317, 321 and 360 fleets

The re-roofed Building 3 at Ilford depot on 19 August 2000.   *Philip Stuart*

57

INVERNESS CARRIAGE SHED
First Scotrail Ltd, Longman Road, Inverness IV1 1RY

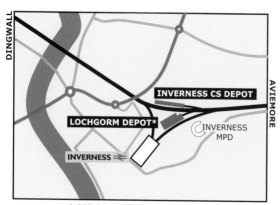

The yard is visible from the line

Directions from Inverness station:
Turn right into Academy Street and third right into Rose Street. Turn left and then right onto Longman Road, cross the railway bridge, turn right into Longman Industrial Estate and right again. This leads to the depot.
(Distance approx 0.6 miles)

* SEE PAGE 59

A 2T dead-ended shed, constructed in brick and corrugated sheeting, with a single-pitch gabled roof, located at NH66914573 and opened in the 1980s by BR as a carriage shed.
Operating company in 2010: First Scotrail
Allocation: Home base for Highland Class 156 and 158 fleets

This general view of the maintenance facilities at Inverness was taken on 14 August 1996. Looking west it shows Lochgorm depot, with Class 08 No 08 754 in the yard on the left and Inverness Carriage Shed depot in the centre. The building on the right was the disused former HR carriage shed.
Philip Stuart

INVERNESS LOCHGORM

First Scotrail Ltd, Diesel Sidings, Inverness Station, Inverness IV1 1LE

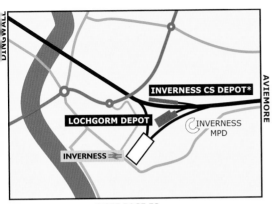

The yard is visible from the line

Directions from Inverness station:
A boarded crossing leads from Platform 5 to the depot.
(Distance approx 200yd)

* SEE PAGE 58

A 4T dead-ended shed, located at NH66954564 and constructed in stone with a twin slated gable-style roof adjoined by a brick-built 2T shed with a corrugated sheeted single-pitched roof. It was converted from the 1864-built ex-Highland Railway Lochgorm Works and opened as a diesel depot by BR in February 1960.

Operating company in 2010: First Scotrail

Allocation: Home base for Highland Class 156 and 158 fleets

Originally built as a locomotive works by the Highland Railway in 1864, it was refurbished and enlarged by BR for diesel use in 1960. Lochgorm depot is viewed here on 14 August 1996.

Philip Stuart

KNOTTINGLEY
Spawd Bone Lane, Knottingley WF11 0JG

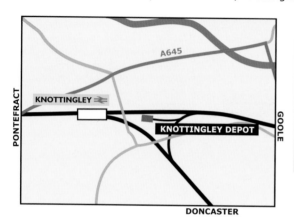

The yard is visible from the line

Directions from Knottingley station:
At the end of the approach road turn right along Pontefract Road, turn right again into Headlands Road and left along Spawd Bone Lane. The depot is on the left.
(Distance approx 800yd)

A 4T servicing shed with one through road, located at SE49332347 and constructed in brick and corrugated sheeting on a steel frame with a gable-style pitched corrugated sheeted roof adjoined by a 1T dead-ended repair shed constructed in brick and corrugated sheeting on a steel frame with a gable-style pitched corrugated sheeted roof. It was opened by BR between 1962 and 1965 and the depot adjoins a 2T through-road wagon works. The allocation was withdrawn from 18 January 1987 and in 2010 the depot was used to service visiting locomotives and shunters.
Operating company in 2010: DB Schenker
Allocation: Nil

Looking west towards Knottingley depot on 15 August 2001.

Philip Stuart

LEEDS MIDLAND ROAD
Freightliner Maintenance Ltd, Midland Road, Hunslet, Leeds LS10 2RJ

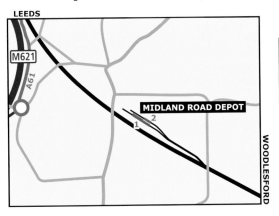

The yard is visible from the line

Directions from Leeds station:
Turn right along New Station Street, right again along Neville Street and turn left into Great Wilson Street. Continue along Hunslet Lane, Hunslet Road and Low Road and turn right into Church Street. Turn left into Balm Road, left into Midland Road and the depot is on the right.
(Distance approx 1.9 miles)

Building 1: A 2T through-road servicing shed, located at SE31223107 and constructed in corrugated sheeting on a steel frame with a glazed and corrugated sheeting-clad gabled single-pitched roof.
Building 2: A 1T through-road fuelling shed, located at SE31263107 and constructed to exactly the same specifications as Building 1.
The depot opened on 11 July 2003 and in 2010 was in use to service Class 66 locomotives and wagons.
Operating company in 2010: Arriva for Freightliner
Allocation: Nil

Leeds Midland Road depot on 31 July 2005. The fuelling shed, Building 2, is on the left and the servicing shed, Building 1, on the right.   *Philip Stuart*

LEEDS NEVILLE HILL
Osmondthorpe Lane, Leeds LS9 9BJ

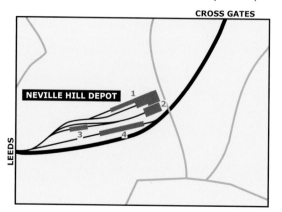

The yard is partially visible from the line

Directions from Leeds station:
Turn right along New Station Street, right into Boar Lane and continue along Duncan Street, Call Lane, New York Street, York Street and Marsh Lane. Turn right along York Road and after about 1.5 miles turn right into Osmondthorpe Lane. The depot is on the right. (Distance approx 2.7 miles)

Building 1: A 4T dead-ended shed, located at SE33083315 and constructed in brick with a glazed and corrugated sheeting-clad multi-pitched gabled roof, adjoined by a 3T dead-ended shed constructed in brick with a corrugated sheeting-clad single-pitched gabled roof. It was originally opened as an in-line 4RH shed by the North Eastern Railway in October 1894 and closed to steam by BR on 12 June 1966. The shed and repair shop were subsequently rebuilt and re-furbished and a 2T extension, constructed in brick with glazed panels and a corrugated sheeting-clad single-pitched gabled roof, was added to the front of the building. In 2010 it was in use by XC for servicing HSTs.

Building 2: A 5T dead-ended shed, located at SE33123310 and constructed in brick and glazed panels with a glazed and corrugated sheeting-clad multi-pitched gab;
Led roof. It was opened by BR in 1960 and slightly extended at the front end in c2000.

Building 3: A 3T through-road shed, located at SE32643300 and constructed in brick and glazed panels with a glazed and corrugated sheeting-clad multi-pitched gabled roof. It was opened by BR in 1960.

Building 4: A 2T through-road shed, located at SE32973300 and constructed in corrugated sheeting on a steel frame with a gable-style single-pitched corrugated sheeted and glazed roof, adjoined by a similarly constructed 1T through-road shed. It was opened in 1979 as an HST and carriage depot.

The depot was opened by BR on 17 June 1960 and electrified on 30 April 1990.

Current operating companies: Cross Country and Northern

Allocation: Home base for Class 321/9 and 333 fleets and Leeds-area DMUs

Building 4, the double 2T shed at Neville Hill depot on 28 July 1991. *Philip Stuart*

LITTLEHAMPTON

Lineside Way, Littlehampton BN17 7EH

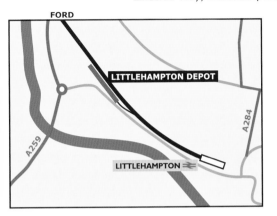

The yard is visible from the line

Directions from Littlehampton station:
Turn left outside of the station, continue along Bridge Road and the depot entrance is a footbridge on the right.
(Distance approx 750yd)

A 3T dead-ended shed, located at TQ01890263 and constructed in brick with a gabled corrugated sheeting-clad and glazed pitched roof. It was opened by the Southern Railway in 1938 and in 2010 was being used to service Class 377 units.
Operating company in 2010: Southern
Allocation: Nil

Littlehampton depot on 11 August 2007 with unit No 377 423 in view. *Philip Stuart*

LIVERPOOL EDGE HILL

Alstom Liverpool Traincare Centre, Picton Rd, Wavertree, Liverpool L15 4LD

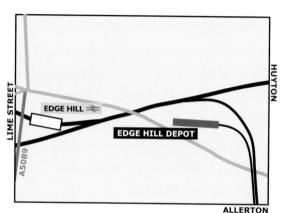

The yard is visible from the line

Directions from Edge Hill station:
Leave the station via the approach road, turn right along Tunnel Road, right into Wavertree Road and continue along Picton Road. The depot is along this road on the left just past the railway bridge. (Distance approx 0.6 miles)

A 2TS dead-ended shed located at SJ37928996 and constructed in corrugated sheeting on a steel frame with a gabled single-pitched corrugated sheeted and glazed roof. It was opened in 2009 to service and maintain Class 390 'Pendolino' units.

Operating company in 2010: Alstom for Virgin West Coast
Allocation: Nil

Edge Hill depot nearing completion on 9 August 2009.

Dave McGuire

LIVERPOOL KIRKDALE

Marsh Street, Kirkdale, Liverpool L20 2BL

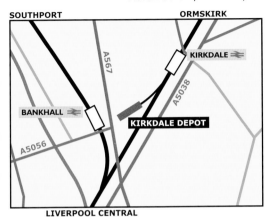

SOUTHPORT

ORMSKIRK

A567

KIRKDALE

A5038

BANKHALL

A5056

KIRKDALE DEPOT

LIVERPOOL CENTRAL

The yard is visible from the line

Directions from Kirkdale station:
Turn left out of the station into Marsh Street and a drive on the left leads to the depot.
(Distance approx 300yd)

A 4T dead-ended shed, located at SJ34639400 and constructed in brick and corrugated sheeting on a steel frame with a corrugated sheeting-clad shallow lean-to-style roof. It occupies the site of the former Bank Hall MPD and was opened by BR in 1977.
Operating company in 2010: Merseyrail
Allocation: Nil

The east end of Kirkdale depot, viewed on 29 June 1992.

Dave McGuire

MACHYNLLETH

Machynlleth Train Care Facility, Heol y Doll, Machynlleth, Powys SY20 8BL

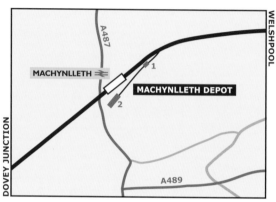

The yard is visible from the line

Directions from Machynlleth station:
A drive leads to the depot from the station yard.
(Distance approx 100yd)

The original steam depot, Building 1, in use as the fuelling shed on 9 June 2009
Paul Smith

Machynlleth MPD, which has occupied the site since 1863, was closed to steam by BR on 5 December 1966 and the two existing buildings, 2TS and 3TS sheds, were given over to servicing DMUs. By 1993 the 3TS building had been demolished.

Building 1: A stone-built 2T through-road shed with a slated gable-style roof located at SH74670148 and opened by the Cambrian Railway at some time prior to 1900. In 2007 it was re-roofed and refurbished as a fuelling shed.

Building 2: A 2T dead-ended shed constructed in corrugated sheeting on a steel frame with a gable-style single-pitched corrugated sheeted and glazed roof. It is located at SH74490126 and was opened by Arriva Trains Wales on 13 August 2007.

Operating company in 2010: Arriva Trains Wales

Allocation: Home base for Cambrian Class 158 sets

The servicing shed, Building 2, at Machynlleth depot on 9 June 2009.   *Paul Smith*

MANCHESTER ARDWICK

Siemens Transportation Systems, Rondin Road, Manchester M12 6BF

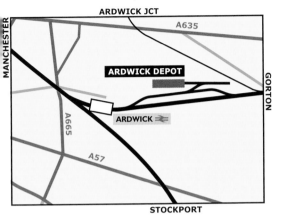

The yard is visible from the line

Directions from Ardwick station:
Turn left out of the station into Blind Lane, right into Chancellor Lane and bear right along Midland Street. Turn right along Ashton Old Road, right into Rondin Lane and the depot is on the right.
(Distance approx 0.7 miles)

A 5T dead-ended shed, located at SJ86369730 and constructed in steel sheeting on a steel frame with a single-pitched steel sheeting-clad roof. It occupies the site of redundant sidings and was opened on 16 May 2006.
Operating company in 2010: Siemens for First TransPennine
Allocation: Home base for Class 185 fleet

The east end of Ardwick depot, viewed on 19 March 2008.   *John Hillmer*

MANCHESTER LONGSIGHT (I)

Alstom, Kirkmanshulme Lane, Manchester M12 4HR

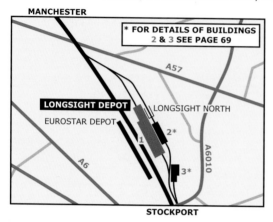

The yard is visible from the line

Directions from Ardwick station:
Turn left outside the station along Blind Lane, left into Devonshire Street North and continue into Devonshire Street. Turn left at the end along Stockport Road, left into Kirkmanshulme Lane and left into Belle Vue Avenue. The depot is at the end of this cul-de-sac.
(Distance approx 1.8 miles)

The site was first used for an engine shed by the Manchester & Birmingham Railway when a small 1RH building was opened here in 1842. By nationalisation it was occupied by Longsight MPD which was composed of two buildings, Longsight North and South, and these formed the original diesel depot. Longsight North was located at SJ86699642 and opened in 1903 by the LNWR. By BR days it was a brick-built 8T shed with one through road and was closed to steam by BR on 14 February 1965. It was then used as a DMU depot but the building was taken out of use in 1994 following partial collapse of the roof. In 2010 the shell of the building was utilised as a stabling area and fuelling point.

Building 1: A brick-built 11T through-road shed with a gable-style multi-pitched roof, it was opened by the LNWR as a carriage shed in c1907. It is located at SJ86689632 and was electrified by BR in 1960 for use as a depot for locomotives and LHCS. By 1990 the easternmost four-track bay had been extended, rebuilt with a high-pitched roof and reduced to two roads.

Operating company in 2010: Alstom for Virgin West Coast
Allocation: Nil

The north end of Longsight depot, viewed on 17 June 1990 and showing Building I and the then-roofed Longsight North MPD housing DMUs.
Philip Stuart

MANCHESTER LONGSIGHT (2&3)
Northern, Kirkmanshulme Lane, Manchester M12 4HR

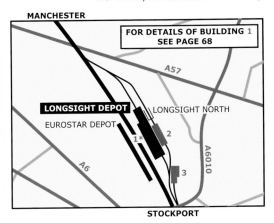

MANCHESTER

FOR DETAILS OF BUILDING 1
SEE PAGE 68

A57

LONGSIGHT DEPOT | LONGSIGHT NORTH

EUROSTAR DEPOT

1*

2

A6

A6010

3

STOCKPORT

The yard is visible from the line

**Directions from
Ardwick station**:
See Page 68

The electric depot, Building 3, at Manchester Longsight depot on 17 June 1990. *Philip Stuart*

Building 2: Longsight South was opened in 1870 by the LNWR. By BR days it was a brick-built 6T dead-ended shed with an LMS-style louvre roof and brick screen, located at SJ86769630. It was closed to steam in 1961.

Building 3: A 2T through-road shed located at SJ86829615 and constructed in brick with a glazed and corrugated sheet single-pitched roof. It was opened by BR on 11 July 1960.

Operating company in 2010: Northern

Allocation: Home base for Manchester Class 323s

Building 2, the former Longsight South MPD, at Longsight depot on 17 June 1990. *Philip Stuart*

69

MANCHESTER NEWTON HEATH

Dean Lane, Manchester M40 3AB

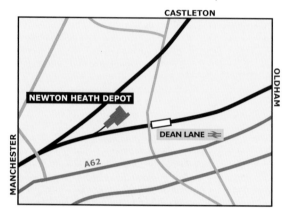

The yard is visible from the Castleton line

Directions from Dean Lane station:
The depot is on the opposite side of the road to the station entrance.
(Distance approx 200yd)

Originally the site of Newton Heath MPD, a 24TS shed located at SD87670090 and opened by the Lancashire & Yorkshire Railway in 1876. In 1959, with the exception of the southernmost 3T bay which was retained for DMU servicing, the southern half of the shed was demolished by BR and a 4T through-road shed, constructed in brick and corrugated sheeting with a glazed and corrugated sheeting-clad single-pitch gabled roof, was subsequently built on the cleared area.

The shed closed to steam on 1 February 1968 and, in 1969, the remaining portion of the steam shed was demolished enabling 1T and 2T through-road sheds, constructed in corrugated sheeting on a steel frame with glazed and corrugated sheeting-clad flat roofs, to be added to the north side of the depot.

Operating company in 2010: Northern
Allocation: Home base for Manchester-area DMUs

Manchester Newton Heath depot on 17 June 1990.

Philip Stuart

MARCH

Network Rail Ltd, March South Down Yard, Station Road, March PE15 8SQ

The yard is visible from the line

Directions from March station:
Leave the station by the approach road, and a drive on the opposite side of Station Road leads to the depot.
(Distance approx 200yd)

Located at TL42139774 and originally constructed by the GER as a brick-built goods shed with a slated gable-style pitched roof. It was refurbished and re-roofed and opened by GBRf as a 1T dead-ended servicing depot on 18 April 2008.

Operating company in 2010: ElectroMotive for GBRf
Allocation: Nil

GBRf Class 66 locomotives Nos 66 727, 66 729 and 66 725 *Sunderland* line up outside of March depot on 18 April 2008, the official opening day.
Richard Gennis

MARGAM

Margam, Nr Port Talbot SA13 2PH

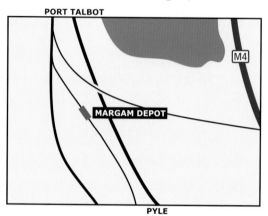

PORT TALBOT

MARGAM DEPOT

PYLE

The yard is partially visible from the line

Directions from Pyle station:
Turn right outside of the station along Pandy Crescent, turn left into Beach Road and bear left along Marlass Road. Cross the railway, turn first right and bear right into Water Street. Pass under the railway line, then turn first left, pass under the motorway, proceed through Kenfig Industrial Estate, and continue under a railway overbridge. This road leads to the depot.
(Distance approx 3.1 miles)

A 2T through-road servicing shed, located at SS79208380 and constructed in brick and corrugated sheeting on a steel frame with a gable-style pitched corrugated sheeted roof, adjoined by a 1T repair shop constructed in brick and corrugated sheeting on a steel frame with a flat roof. It was officially opened by BR on 30 December 1963 but did not become fully operational until June 1965. In 2010 it was used for servicing shunters and visiting locomotives.

Operating company in 2010: DB Schenker
Allocation: Nil

Margam depot, looking north west on 22 May 1997 with Class 56 No 56 119 inside and Class 56 and 37 locomotives stabled alongside.
Philip Stuart

MEREHEAD

Merehead Quarry, East Cranmore, Somerset BA4 4SQ

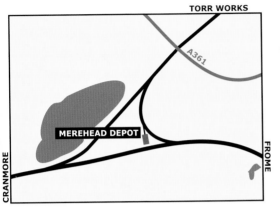

Passenger trains do not operate along this line

Directions from Cranmore West (East Somerset Railway) station: Turn left at the end of the station approach road and first right along East Cranmore Lane. At East Cranmore turn left into Turnpike Lane and then right into the A361. The depot entrance is along this road, on the right just after a railway bridge.
(Distance approx 3.6 miles)
(NB: The distance to the nearest BR-operated station [Frome] is 5.5 miles)

A 3T dead-ended shed, located at ST69094323 and constructed in corrugated sheeting on a steel frame with a gable-style single-pitched corrugated sheeted and glazed roof. It was opened by Foster Yeoman in 1980 and incorporated a wagon works. The shed was rebuilt in 1985.
Operating company in 2010: Mendip Rail
Allocation: Home base for Class 59 locomotives and wagons

Merehead depot on 26 June 1991 with Class 08 No 08 032 and Class 59 No 59 003 in the yard.
Philip Stuart

MOUNTSORREL

Lafarge Aggregates Ltd, Sileby Road, Barrow upon Soar, Loughborough LE12 8LX

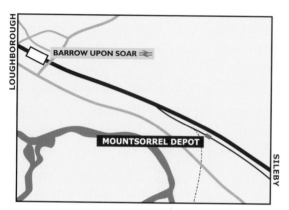

The yard is visible from the line

Directions from Barrow upon Soar station: Turn right outside of the station along Grove Lane, left into Sileby Road and the entrance to the quarry yard is on the left. The depot is in the yard.
(Distance approx 0.8 miles)

A 1T through-road fuelling shed, located at SK58591681 and constructed in corrugated sheeting on a steel frame with a corrugated sheeting-clad single-pitched gabled roof. It was opened by EWS in 2001 for the Leicester stone traffic.
Operating company in 2010: DB Schenker
Allocation: Nil

EWS Class 60 No 66 176 stabling inside the small shed building at Mountsorrel depot on 18 February 2007.
Nick Pigott

NEWCASTLE HEATON

Benfield Road, Heaton, Newcastle upon Tyne NE6 4NU

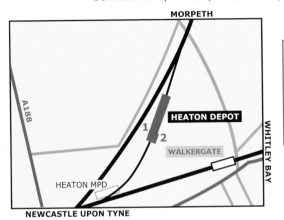

The yard is visible from the line

Directions from Walkergate (Metro) station: Turn left out of the station along Benfield Road and the depot is on the left, just before a railway bridge.
(Distance approx 0.7 miles)

Building 1: A 7T shed located at NZ27916598 and composed of a 4T through-road shed constructed in brick with a gable-style corrugated sheeting-clad and glazed pitched roof, and a 3T shed, with one through road, of similar construction

Building 2: A 1T brick-built shed with a flat roof, located at NZ27896585 and adjoining the main shed at the south east corner.

The depot was opened by BR on 7 November 1977 and is built on the site of carriage sidings.

Operating company in 2010: Northern

Allocation: Home base for Northeastern DMUs and Grand Central HSTs

Newcastle Heaton depot on 20 August 1989.

Philip Stuart

NEW CROSS GATE

London Overground, Surrey Canal Road, London SE14 5RT

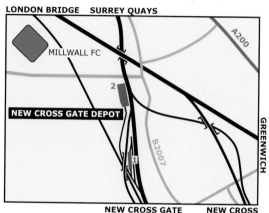

The yard is visible from the Surrey Quays line and partially visible from the London Bridge line

Directions from New Cross Gate station: A fenced footpath leads to the depot from the north end of Platform 5.
(Distance approx 600yd)

Building 1: A 2T through-road shed located at TQ35957758 and consisting of two adjoining 1T buildings constructed in sheeting on a steel frame with sheeting-clad and glazed lean-to-style roofs.

Building 2: A 4T dead-ended shed, located at TQ35937789 and constructed in sheeting and glazed panels on a steel frame with a glazed and sheeting-clad flat roof.

The depot was built in connection with the transfer of the East London line from Underground to Overground and was due to open in 2010.

Operating company in 2010: London Overground

Allocation: Class 378 units

New Cross Gate depot under construction on 21 April 2009. This view, from the south end of the yard, shows Building 1 on the left and the 4T Building 2 in the near distance.   *Nick Pigott*

76

NORTHAMPTON KINGS HEATH

Siemens Transportation Systems, Heathfield Way, Kings Heath, Northampton NN5 7QP

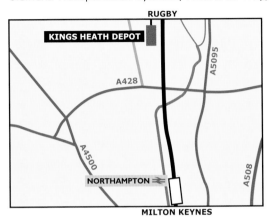

The yard is visible from the line

Directions from Northampton station: Turn left outside of the station along St Andrew's Road, turn left along Spencer Bridge Road, cross the bridge and turn right along Gladstone Road. Turn right into Heathfield Way and the depot entrance is along this road on the right.
(Distance approx 1.5 miles)

A 5T dead-ended shed, located at SP74596132 and constructed in corrugated sheeting on a steel frame with a gable-style single-pitched corrugated sheeted and glazed roof. It was opened on 27 June 2006.
Operating company in 2010: Siemens for London & Birmingham
Allocation: Home base for Class 350 fleet

The north end of Kings Heath depot, viewed on 27 June 2006, the official opening day.
Chris Milner

NORWICH CROWN POINT
Crown Point Depot, Hardy Road, Norwich NR1 1JR

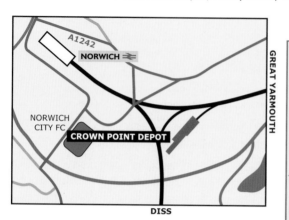

The yard is visible from the line

Directions from Norwich station:
Turn right outside of the station along Thorpe Road, turn right into Lower Clarence Road and right again along Clarence Road. Turn right into Carrow Road, cross over the railway and descend into Hardy Road via the steps on the left. Continue along this road and the depot entrance is on the left-hand side, just past the railway bridge.
(Distance approx 1.1 miles)

A depot complex located at TG24640788 and composed of adjoining 1T through-road, 2T dead-ended, 1T dead-ended and 1T and 2T through-road sheds all similarly constructed in brick and corrugated sheeting with glazed and corrugated sheeting-clad single-pitch gabled roofs.

The depot was opened by BR on 27 October 1982 and electrified in May 1987.

Operating company in 2010: National Express East Anglia

Allocation: Home base for Class 90 locomotives and stock and East Anglian DMUs

The north end of Crown Point depot, viewed on 27 July 1995 with Class 08 No 08 810 in the yard.
Philip Stuart

NOTTINGHAM EASTCROFT

East Midlands Trains Ltd, London Rd, Nottingham NG2 3AH

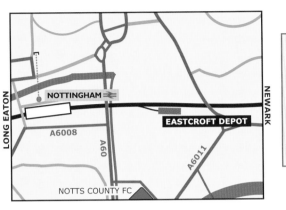

The yard is visible from the line

Directions from Nottingham station:
Turn left outside of the station along Carrington Street and left into Queen's Road. Continue into Eastcroft and the depot entrance is along this road.
(Distance approx 0.5 miles)

A 2T through-road shed, located at SK58223922 and constructed in corrugated sheeting and glazed panels on a steel frame with a single-pitched corrugated sheet-clad roof. It was officially opened by Central Trains on 7 May 1999 and, in 2010, serviced Class 156, 158 and 170 units.
Operating company in 2010: East Midlands Trains
Allocation: Nil

Nottingham Eastcroft depot on 9 October 1999 with Unit No 170 510 in the yard. *Philip Stuart*

79

OLD OAK COMMON

Old Oak Common Lane, Willesden, London NW10 6DQ

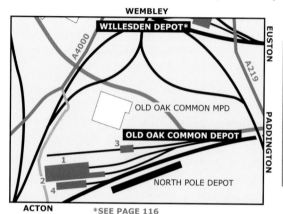

The yard is visible from the line

**Directions from
Willesden Junction
(Low Level) station:**
Turn right outside of the
station along the approach
road, turn left into Old Oak
Lane and left again along Old
Oak Common Lane.
The depots are on the left.
(Distance approx 0.7 miles)

*SEE PAGE 116

OLD OAK COMMON CARRIAGE SHED & HST DEPOT

Building 1: A 15T dead-ended shed located at TQ21508205 and constructed in brick with a gable-style corrugated sheeting-clad triple-pitched roof. It was originally constructed as a 30T carriage shed by the GWR but the northern half was demolished by BR and the remainder given over to DMU servicing, replacing Southall from 1986.

Building 2: A 3T dead-ended shed, located at TQ21488200 and constructed in corrugated sheeting on a steel frame with a glazed and corrugated sheeting-clad single-pitched gabled roof. It was opened by BR as an HST depot in December 1976.

Building 3: A 3T through-road shed, located at TQ21798216 and constructed to the same specifications as Building 2. It was opened by First Great Western on 26 July 2002.

Operating company in 2010: First Great Western

Allocation: Home base for Class 57/6 fleet and HSTs

OLD OAK COMMON HEATHROW EXPRESS

Building 4: A 3T dead-ended shed, located at TQ21478197 and constructed to the same specifications as Buildings 2 and 3. It was opened on 14 September 1997.

Operating company in 2010: Siemens for Heathrow Express

Allocation: Home base for Class 332 and 360 fleets

Old Oak Common (Heathrow Express) depot (Building 4) on 20 April 2005 with Class 360 units Nos 201 and 203 parked alongside. *Chris Milner*

PENZANCE LONG ROCK

Long Road, Penzance TR20 8HT

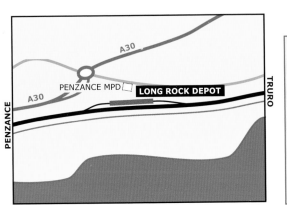

PENZANCE

A30

PENZANCE MPD

LONG ROCK DEPOT

A30

TRURO

The yard is visible from the line

Directions from Penzance station:
Turn right outside of the station into Station Road, right into Chyandour Cliff and continue along Eastern Green. At the second roundabout turn right towards Long Rock and, at the next roundabout, turn right again. The depot is along this road, on the left.
(Distance approx 1.4 miles)

A 1T through-road shed, located at SW49283122 and constructed in brick and corrugated sheeting with a single-pitch gable-style roof with two similarly constructed 1T lean-to-style through-road fuelling sheds attached to the south side. It was located slightly to the south of the site of Penzance MPD and was opened by BR in 1977. It probably saw use as a carriage shed until HST operations began in August 1979, and in 2010 was also used to service Class 57 locomotives and sleeper stock.
Operating company in 2010: First Great Western
Allocation: Nil

Looking east at Penzance Long Rock depot on 10 July 2008 with the main line on the right and a salt water-corroded near-roofless 1T fuelling shed attached to the main building.   *Philip Stuart*

PERTH

Caledonian Road, Perth PH2 8HF

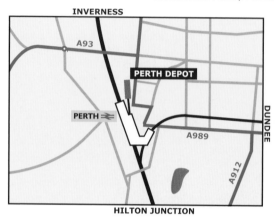

The depot is not visible from the line

Directions from Perth station:
Leave by the main exit, bear left into Leonard Street and turn left along St Andrew Street. Turn right into Caledonian Road and the depot is on the left.
(Distance approx 300yd)

An 8T through-road building located at NO11222335 and opened by the Caledonian Railway as a carriage shed prior to 1901. It is constructed with corrugated sheeting screens, cut short above ground level and mounted on cast-iron columns, with a corrugated sheeting-clad transverse multi-pitched roof. It was used by BR for stabling DMUs from c1960.

Operating company in 2010: First Scotrail
Allocation: Nil

The south end of Perth depot on 18 August 1996 with unit No 117 310 in view to the right of the building.
Philip Stuart

PETERBOROUGH

1A Mayors Walk, Peterborough PE1 2AD

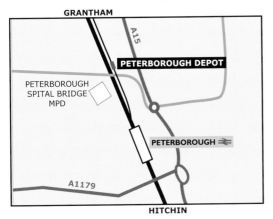

The yard is visible from the line

Directions from Peterborough station:
Turn left outside of the station into Station Road, left along Bourges Boulevard and left at the roundabout into Mayors Walk. A road on the left-hand side leads to the depot.
(Distance approx 500yd)

A 1T through-road shed, located at TL18509932 and constructed in brick and glazed panels on a steel frame with a single-pitched corrugated sheeting-clad roof. It was opened by BR on 9 March 1969 and in 2010 was in use to service visiting locomotives and DMUs.

Operating company in 2010: DB Schenker
Allocation: Nil

Peterborough depot on 22 October 2008 with EWS Class 66 No 66 030 parked alongside.

Nick Pigott

PETERBOROUGH NEW ENGLAND

GBRf, Maskew Avenue, Peterborough PE1 2AS

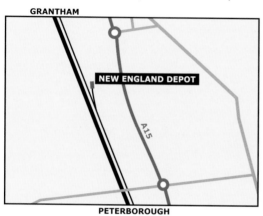

The yard is visible from the line

Directions from Peterborough station:
Turn left outside of the station into Station Road and left along Bourges Boulevard. At the third roundabout turn left into Maskew Avenue and the depot entrance is a roadway on the left.
(Distance approx 1.4 miles)

A 1T dead-ended shed, located at TF18100035 and constructed in corrugated sheeting on a steel frame with a single-pitched roof. It was originally built by BR in 1987 for use as an overhead line maintenance depot and was opened as a diesel shed in 2001 by GBRf. In 2010 it was in use to service visiting Class 66 and 73 locomotives.
Operating company in 2010: GBRf
Allocation: Nil

The north end of New England depot, viewed on 22 October 2008.   *Nick Pigott*

84

PLYMOUTH LAIRA

Embankment Road, Plymouth PL4 9JN

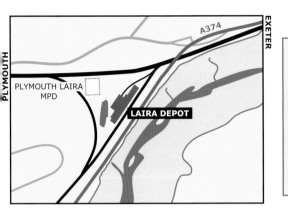

The yard is visible from the line

Directions from Plymouth station:
Turn right outside of the station and, at the end of the approach road, turn left along Saltash Road. Continue along Cobourg Street, Charles Street, Exeter Street and Embankment Road.
The depot is on the left.
(Distance approx 2.4 miles)

Originally a 9T shed constructed in concrete with a high Dutch barn-style roof over the central 2T dead-ended repair shop, and transverse Dutch barn-style roofs over the 4T dead-ended west bay and 3T through-road east bay. It is located at SX50485562 and was opened by BR in December 1961.

In 1981 the eastern 3T bay was demolished and replaced with a 3T through-road shed constructed in brick and glazed panels on a steel frame with a single-pitched corrugated sheet-clad gabled roof. It was opened on 30 September 1981 by BR to accommodate HSTs.

A 1T through-road shed constructed in brick and glazed panels on a steel frame with a single shallow-pitched corrugated sheet-clad gabled roof was added on the east side in November 1993 for the EPNS.

Operating company in 2010: First Great Western
Allocation: Home base for HSTs

The classic 1960s style of architecture of Laira depot was looking pretty weary when viewed on 27 July 1997. Class 08 shunters Nos 08 645 and 08 648 were in the yard. *Philip Stuart*

RAMSGATE

Newington Road, Ramsgate CT12 6EE

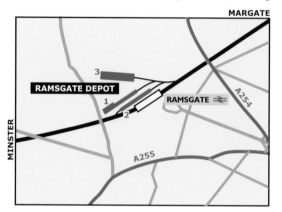

MARGATE

RAMSGATE DEPOT

RAMSGATE ≷

A254

A255

MINSTER

The yard is visible from the line and the station

Directions from Ramsgate station:
Turn right along the approach road, right into Wilfred Road and right along a footpath. At the end turn right along Newington Road, cross the railway bridge and the depot is on the right.
(Distance approx 600yd)

Building 1: Originally a 6T dead-ended shed, located at TR37056569 and constructed in concrete with an eastlight-pattern roof. It was built by the SR in September 1930 and closed to steam by BR in December 1960. The two-track section on the southern side was demolished, a new brick wall installed, and an extension constructed in brick and corrugated sheeting on a steel frame with a glazed and corrugated sheeting-clad gabled single-pitched roof was added to the eastern end to accommodate EMUs.

Building 2: A 4T through-road shed, located at TR37206573 and constructed in corrugated sheeting on a steel frame with a glazed and corrugated sheeting-clad gabled single-pitched roof. It was opened by the SR as a carriage shed and converted to EMU use in c1960.

Building 3: A 5T dead-ended shed located at TR37036584 and constructed in corrugated sheeting on a steel frame with a glazed and corrugated sheeting-clad lean-to-style roof. It was opened by South Eastern in 2009 to service Class 395 units.

Operating company in 2010: South Eastern
Allocation: Home base for Class 375 fleet

The east end of Ramsgate depot, viewed on 12 May 1990 with Building 2 on the left and Building 1, the extended former steam shed, on the right. *Philip Stuart*

86

READING

Cow Lane, Reading RG1 8NA

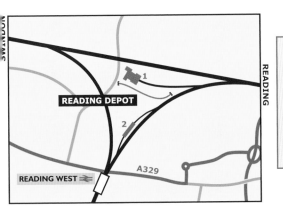

The yard is visible from all lines

**Directions from
Reading West station**:
Turn left outside of the station
into Oxford Road and right
along Salisbury Road. Turn
right at the end into Cow Lane
and the entrance is on the
right.
(Distance approx 0.6 miles)

Building 1: A 3T dead-ended shed, located at SU70437395 and constructed in brick and corrugated sheeting with a glazed and corrugated sheeting-clad single-pitch gable roof. It was built at the west end of the former shed yard of Reading (GWR) MPD and opened by BR in 1961. A 2T dead-ended shed constructed in brick and corrugated sheeting with a corrugated sheeting-clad single-pitch gable roof was added on the south side in 1964 and extended at the east end in 1983.

Building 2: A 2T through-road shed, located at SU70377367 and constructed in brick and corrugated sheeting with a corrugated sheeting-clad single-pitch gable roof. It was officially opened on 8 March 1991 by Thames Trains.

Operating company in 2010: First Great Western

Allocation: Home base for Class 165 and 166 fleets

Building 2 under construction at Reading depot on 6 October 1990.   *Philip Stuart*

RUGBY

Colas Rail, Rail Plant Depot, Mill Road, Rugby CV21 1BE

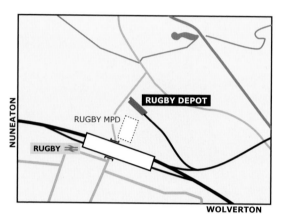

The yard is not visible from the line

**Directions from
Rugby station**:
Turn left along Station
Terrace, left into Murray Road
and continue along Mill Road.
The entrance is on the right.
(Distance approx 700yd)

Originally a brick-built 3T dead-ended workshop located at SP51287619 and opened by
the LNWR in November 1892 as a division of Crewe Works. It closed in July 1959 and
BR subsequently partially demolished it (retaining the south wall) and rebuilt it in brick
and sheeting on a steel frame with a glazed and corrugated sheeting-clad single-pitched
roof. It then re-opened in early 1963 as a traction maintenance depot, was transferred
to the Civil Engineers Department in 1969 and later privatised. By 2009 it was in use as
a rail plant and locomotive depot for Colas Rail.
Operating company in 2010: Colas Rail
Allocation: Nil

Colas Rail Class 47s Nos 47 739 *Robin of Templecombe* & 47 727 parked outside of Rugby depot.
John Groocock

RYDE

St John's Road, Ryde, Isle of Wight PO33 2BA

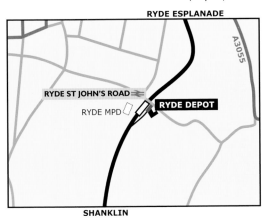

The yard is visible from the line

**Directions from
Ryde St John's Rd station**:
Ascend the steps outside of
the station, turn right along St
John's Road and the depot is
on the right.
(Distance approx 200yd)

A 2T dead-ended shed located at SZ59649194 and constructed in corrugated sheeting on a steel frame with a corrugated sheeting-clad and glazed transverse triple-pitched roof. It was originally built as a carriage shop by the Southern Railway and opened as an EMU depot by BR on 20 March 1967, the first day of electrified operations on the island.

Operating company in 2010: Island Line
Allocation: Home base for Class 483 fleet

Ryde depot on 18 January 2008.

Chris Milner

ST BLAZEY

St Blazey Road, Par PL24 2HY

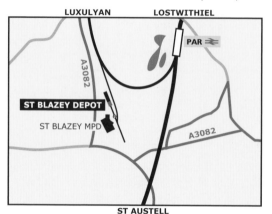

The yard is not visible from the line

Directions from Par station:
Turn right outside of the station along a footpath and continue along Moorland Road. At the end of the road turn right under a railway bridge, proceed over the level crossing and turn right along Harbour Road. Turn right into St Blazey Road and the depot is on the right.
(Distance approx 1.0 mile)

A 2T dead-ended shed, located at SX07345383 and constructed in corrugated sheeting and glazed panels on a steel frame with a single-pitched corrugated sheet-clad roof. It is open along the west side and adjoins the front of the former 3TS wagon works. These works were originally built by the Cornwall Mineral Railway as a steam shed, re-opened as a diesel depot by BR on 25 April 1987 to replace the now-listed former BR St Blazey MPD and later closed for locomotive use. In 2010 the depot was in use as a fuelling and servicing point for visiting locomotives.

Operating company in 2010: DB Schenker
Allocation: 1 x Class 09 shunter (09 016)

A weed-strewn St Blazey depot on 14 June 2009 with Class 66 No 66 237 stabling under the canopy.
Keith Batchelor

ST LEONARDS

Bridgeway, St Leonards on Sea TN38 8AP

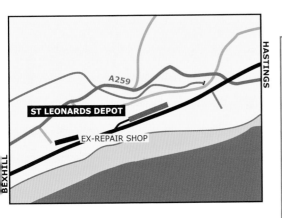

The yard is visible from the line

**Directions from
West St Leonards station**:
Turn right outside of the
station along St Vincents Road
and left at the end into
Filsham Road. Continue along
Bulverhythe Road, turn left
into Arnside Road, right into
Cliftonville Road and the
entrance is along this road on
the left.
(Distance approx 0.7 miles)
NB: Vehicular access is via
Bridgeway, off Bexhill Road about
500yd to the west.

A 5T dead-ended shed, located at TQ78000865
and constructed in brick with a gable-style corrugated sheeting-clad and glazed pitched roof. It
was opened by BR as a DEMU depot in March 1957 and electrified in 1986. In 2010 it
was in use for the servicing of Class 377 units.
Operating company in 2010: Southern
Allocation: Nil

St Leonards depot on 17 June 1989 with unit No 205 008 in the yard.   *Philip Stuart*

SALISBURY FISHERTON YARD

Fisherton Street, Salisbury SP2 7DX

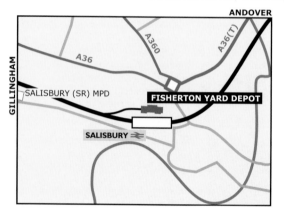

The yard is partially visible from the line and the station

Directions from Salisbury station:
Turn left outside of the station into South Western Road, left into Fisherton Street and left again along Windsor Road. The depot is on the left.
(Distance approx 200yd)

A 3T dead-ended shed, located at SU13673024 and constructed in corrugated sheeting on steel frames with a glazed and corrugated sheeting-clad lean-to-style roof. Two 1T through-road sheds, similarly constructed, were attached to the south side.
The depot was opened by Network SouthEast in 1993.
Operating company in 2010: South West Trains
Allocation: Home base for Class 159 fleet

The west end of Fisherton Yard depot, viewed on 6 July 2005.   *Chris Milner*

SELHURST

Selhurst Train Maintenance Depot, Selhurst Road, London SE25 6LJ

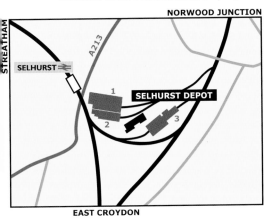

NORWOOD JUNCTION

STREATHAM

A213

SELHURST

SELHURST DEPOT

1

2

3

EAST CROYDON

The yard is partially visible from the line

Directions from Selhurst station:
The depot is on the opposite side of the road to the station entrance.
(Distance approx 200yd)

The depot was originally opened by the London, Brighton & South Coast Railway in 1911 when a 6T shed was built for its overhead electric stock. This became a paint shop in 1911 and was demolished in 2000.

Building 1: A 9T dead-ended shed located at TQ33256756 and constructed in corrugated sheeting on a steel frame with a glazed and corrugated sheeting-clad triple-pitched gable roof. It was built on the site of 'The Nest' a former ground of Crystal Palace FC and opened as a 12T building in 1928 by the SR. It was reduced by three roads when the depot was refurbished and modernised in 2002-5.

Building 2: A 5T dead-ended shed located at TQ33256749 and constructed in brick and corrugated sheeting on a steel frame with a glazed and corrugated sheeting-clad multi-pitched gable roof. It was opened by BR in 1958 and utilised as a Level 5 depot between 1987 and 1993.

Building 3: A 7T through-road shed located at TQ33556744 and constructed of corrugated sheeting on a steel frame with a gable-style corrugated sheeted and glazed single-pitched roof. It was opened by NSE Thameslink on 9 September 1986.

Operating company in 2010: Southern

Allocation: Home base for Class 171, 319, 377, 455 and 456 fleets

Building 3, the Thameslink shed at Selhurst depot on 16 October 1999.   *Philip Stuart*

SHEFFIELD SHREWSBURY ROAD

Fish Dock, Suffolk Road, Sheffield S2 4AF

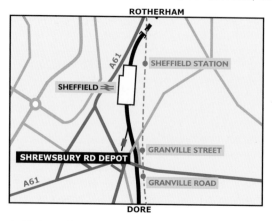

The yard is partially visible from both the line and the station

Directions from Sheffield station:
Turn left outside of the station along Cross Turner Street and continue into Fornham Street. Turn left into Suffolk Road and the depot is on the left.
(Distance approx 400yd)

A 1T through-road shed, located at SK35848645 and constructed in concrete blocks and corrugated sheeting on a steel frame with a corrugated sheeting-clad single-pitch gable roof. It was opened by BR in c1987 and in 2010 was in use as a fuelling shed for visiting DMUs.

Operating company in 2010: Northern
Allocation: Nil

It seems astonishing that a city that once boasted a concentration of some of the largest steam sheds in the country, Darnall, Grimesthorpe and Millhouses, succeeded by the massive Tinsley TMD, should now be reduced to a basic 1T fuelling shed for visiting DMUs. Sheffield Shrewsbury Road depot is seen here on 11 August 1991.
Philip Stuart

SHREWSBURY COLEHAM YARD

Network Rail Ltd, Coleham Depot, Betton Street, Shrewsbury SY3 7LJ

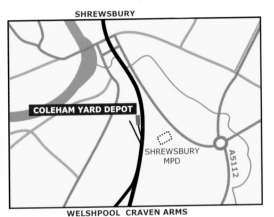

The yard is visible from the line

Directions from Shrewsbury station:
Turn left along Castle Gates, continue along the A5191, bear right into Dogpole and turn left along Wyle Cop. Cross the river bridge, turn right into Coleham Head and the depot entrance is on the left-hand side of the junction with Old Coleham and Betton Street.
(Distance approx 0.9 miles)

A 1T dead-ended shed located at SJ49891198 and constructed of corrugated sheeting on a steel frame with a Dutch barn-style corrugated sheeted and glazed roof. It was opened on 20 May 2009 to maintain and service the ERTMS pilot locomotives used on the Cambrian Line during re-signalling work.

Operating company in 2010: Network Rail
Allocation: 3 x Class 97 locomotives

Coleham Yard depot, complete with its own steel security fence, on 9 September 2009.

Paul Smith

SLADE GREEN
Slade Green Maintenance Depot, Moat Lane, Erith DA8 2NJ

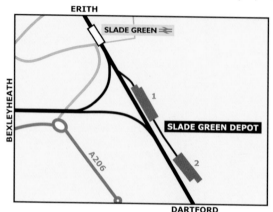

The yard is visible from the line

**Directions from
Slade Green station**:
Leave the station and the
depot entrance is on the right.
(Distance approx 200yd)

Building 1: An 8T through-road shed, located at TQ52507623 and constructed in brick
with a glazed and corrugated sheeting-clad shallow single-pitch gable roof adjoined by
a 2T dead-ended shed constructed in brick with a corrugated sheeting-clad lean-to-style
roof. It was originally built by the South Eastern & Chatham Railway in 1901 and closed
to steam by the SR in 1926. The building was converted to an EMU depot and extended
at the north end by BR in 1959.

Building 2: An 8T dead-ended shed, located at TQ52747588 and constructed in
corrugated sheeting and glazed panels on a steel frame with a glazed and corrugated
sheeting-clad multi-pitched gable roof.

It was originally built by the SR in c1926 as a 10T dead-ended EMU repair shop and was
refurbished as an 8T depot, with extensions over six of the tracks, by Network
SouthEast. It officially re-opened on 8 April 1991.

Operating company in 2010: South Eastern

Allocation: Home base for Class 376, 465 and 466 fleets

The south end of Building 1, the former SE&CR steam shed, at Slade Green depot on 3 March 1993
Dave McGuire

SOUTHAMPTON MARITIME

Southampton Maritime Freightliner Terminal, Dock Gate 20, Western Dock Extension,
Southampton SO15 0LJ

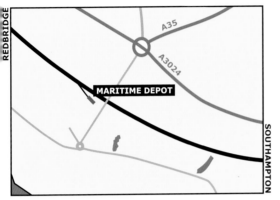

The yard is visible from the line

**Directions from
Redbridge station**:
At the end of the approach
road turn right into Old
Redbridge Road and continue
along Redbridge Road. At the
roundabout turn right along
First Avenue and Dock Gate
20, the entrance to the
Terminal, is at the end.
(Distance approx 0.9 miles)

A 1T through-road shed, located at SU38011296 and constructed in concrete blocks and
corrugated sheeting on a steel frame with a glazed and corrugated sheeting-clad
single-pitch gable roof. It was originally opened as a wagon shop in c1996 and used as
a servicing shed for Freightliner locomotives from c2003.
Operating company in 2010: Freightliner
Allocation: Nil

Southampton Maritime depot, viewed on 6 May 2003. *Philip Stuart*

SOUTHAMPTON NORTHAM

Siemens Northam Traincare Facility, Radcliffe Road, Southampton SO14 0PS

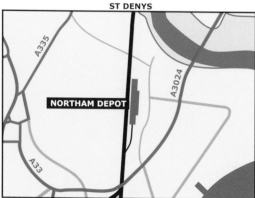

The yard is visible from the line

Directions from St Denys station:
Turn right outside of the station along the approach road and right into Adelaide Road. Turn right into Priory Road, continue along Dukes Road, turn left into Empress Road and continue along Imperial Road. Turn left at the end into Pleasant Road, right into Radcliffe Road and the depot is on the right.
(Distance approx 0.7 miles)

A 4T dead-ended shed, located at SU42881258 and constructed in corrugated sheeting on a steel frame with a gable-style single-pitched corrugated sheeted and glazed roof. It was opened on 2 July 2003 and occupies the site of Northam shed and yard which was built by the L&SWR in October 1840 and closed in January 1901.

Operating company in 2010: Siemens for South West Trains
Allocation: Home base for Class 444 and 450 fleets

Southampton Northam depot nearing completion on 6 May 2003.   *Philip Stuart*

STAVELEY BARROW HILL

Barrow Hill Roundhouse Centre, Campbell Drive, Staveley, Chesterfield S43 2PR

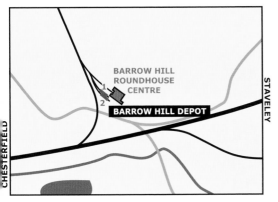

The yard is not visible from the line

Directions from Chesterfield station:
Leave along Malkin Street, turn right into Brimington Road and right into Chesterfield Road. Continue along Church Street and Ringwood Road and turn left into Private Drive. Turn left along Works Road, right into Campbell Drive and the entrance is on the left.
(Distance approx 3.8 miles)

Building 1: A 2T shed with one through road, located at SK41257547 and constructed in corrugated sheeting on a steel frame with a gable-style single-pitched corrugated sheeted and glazed roof.

Building 2: A 2T through-road shed, located at SK41257546 and constructed in similar fashion to Building 1

The depot opened in 2004 and both of the buildings are constructed with a brick screen façade at the south end to keep them in context with the listed roundhouse alongside.

Operating company in 2010: Barrow Hill Ltd

Allocation: Nil

The south end of Barrow Hill depot, viewed on 5 October 2004. The brick façade is clearly visible with Building 2 on the left and Building I on the right.   *Nick Pigott*

99

STEWARTS LANE

Stewarts Lane Depot, St Rule Street, London SW8 3EL

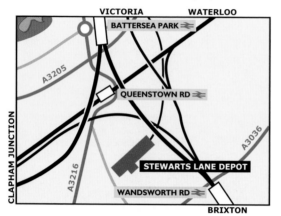

The yard is visible from the high-level Battersea Park—Wandsworth Road line

Directions from Wandsworth Road station: Turn left outside of the station along Wandsworth Road, second right into St Rule Street and the depot is at the end of this road.
(Distance approx 600 yards)

A 14T dead-ended shed located at TQ28937641 and constructed in brick and corrugated sheeting on a steel frame with a transverse multi-pitched corrugated sheeted and glazed roof. It was opened by BR in 1959 and incorporated part of the original Longhedge Works at the rear.

Operating company in 2010: Southern
Allocation: Home base for Class 460 fleet

Stewarts Lane depot on 25 July 1989. The building at the rear is the original Longhedge Works which were opened by the London, Chatham & Dover Railway in 1862. *Philip Stuart*

STOKE LONGPORT

Brookside, Longport, Stoke-on-Trent ST6 4NF

The yard is visible from the line

**Directions from
Longport station**:
Turn left outside of the station along Station Street, first left into Brookside and the entrance is at the end of this cul-de-sac.
(Distance approx 120yd)

A 2T dead-ended shed located at SJ85554957 and constructed in sheeting on a steel frame with a glazed and sheeting-clad single-pitch gable roof. It was originally built as a wagon works and taken over by ElectroMotive in 2008 to maintain and service Class 66 locomotives.
Operating company in 2010: ElectroMotive
Allocation: Nil

The north end of Longport depot, viewed on 26 December 2009.   Paul Smith

STOURBRIDGE JUNCTION
Stourbridge Junction Station, Chawn Hill, Stourbridge DY9 7JD

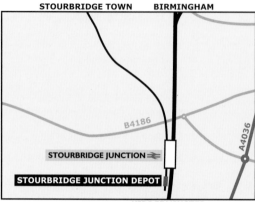

The depot is visible from the line

> **Directions from Stourbridge Junction station**:
> Entrance is effected from the station platform.
> (Distance approx 50yd)

A 1T through-road shed, located at SO90968317 and constructed of concrete blocks and glazed panels with a corrugated sheeting-clad single-pitch gable roof. It was opened by London Midland in 2009.
Operating company in 2010: London Midland
Allocation: Home base for Class 139 units

Stourbridge Junction depot on 28 March 2009, two days after the two Parry Peoplemover units had been approved to take over the working of the Stourbridge Town branch. Class 139 unit No 139 002 is seen here undergoing final tests and driver training before the service was launched, initially on Saturdays and Sundays throughout April, culminating in a total takeover on 17 May 2009.
Paul Smith

STRAWBERRY HILL

Strawberry Hill Depot, Shacklegate Lane, Teddington TW11 8SF

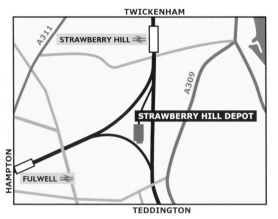

The yard is partially visible from all of the lines

Directions from Strawberry Hill station: Turn left outside of the station and immediately right into Strawberry Hill Road. Turn right at the end along Waldegrave Road, right into Shacklegate Lane and the depot entrance is on the right. (Distance approx 0.5 miles)

A brick-built 9T dead-ended shed with four corrugated sheeting-clad pitched roofs and glazed gables, located at TQ15447200 and closed to steam by the SR. It was originally opened as an engine shed by the L&SWR in 1897 and converted to an EMU depot in 1923. The western 3T section of the depot was abandoned by BR CM&EE in March 1996 when its role in rolling stock development ceased, but was reinstated by Siemens in 2007 to commission new stock. The eastern side remained in use for EMUs and in 2010 was used for servicing Class 450 and 455 units.

Operating company in 2010: South West Trains
Allocation: Nil

Strawberry Hill depot on 19 July 1989. *Philip Stuart*

STREATHAM HILL

Drewstead Road, Streatham Hill SW16 1AB

The yard is visible from the line

Directions from Streatham Hill station: Turn right outside of the station into Streatham Hill, right into Drewstead Road and the depot is on the right. (Distance approx 600yd)

An 8T dead-ended shed, located at TQ29807278 and constructed in corrugated sheeting on a steel frame with a corrugated sheeting-clad twin-gable pitched roof. It was opened by the SR in *c*1937 and in 2010 was used to service Class 377 units.

Operating company in 2010: Southern

Allocation: Nil

The west end of Streatham Hill depot, viewed on 8 June 1989.   *Philip Stuart*

SWANSEA LANDORE

Neath Road, Landore, Swansea SA1 2LQ

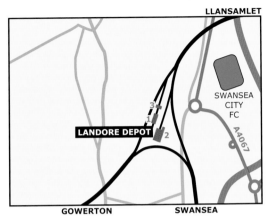

The yard is visible from the line

Directions from Swansea station: Turn right along High Street, bear right into Prince of Wales Road and continue over the footbridge spanning New Cut Road. Bear left at the end, and at the end of the path turn right along Neath Road. The depot is along this road on the left.
(Distance approx 0.9 miles)

Originally the site of Landore MPD which was opened by the GWR in 1874 and closed to steam by BR on 11 June 1961. The shed was demolished by 1963.

Building 1: A 3T through-road servicing shed, located at SS65829529 and constructed in brick and corrugated sheeting on a steel frame with a northlight-pattern corrugated sheet-clad roof.

Building 2: A 4T dead-ended maintenance shed, located at SS65849521 and constructed in brick and corrugated sheeting on a steel and concrete frame with a twin-gable glazed and corrugated sheet-clad roof.

Building 3: A 3T through-road fuelling shed, located at SS65859537 and constructed in brick with a flat roof.

The depot was opened by BR on 3 May 1963 and was designed to accommodate an allocation of 175 locomotives, but by 1989 only a few shunters remained.

In 2010 the depot was in use for the servicing of DMUs and HSTs.

Operating company in 2010: First Great Western

Allocation: Nil

Looking south towards Building 2, the high-bay 4T maintenance shed, at Landore depot on 19 June 1986.
Dave McGuire

TEMPLE MILLS

Eurostar UK Ltd, 2 Orient Way, London E10 5YA

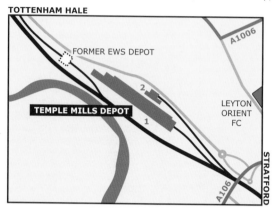

The yard is visible from the line

Directions from Leyton (LT) Station:
Turn right outside of the station along High Road and left into Maud Road. At the end turn left along Ruckholt Road and second right into Orient Way. The depot is along this road on the left.
(Distance approx 0.9 miles)

Building 1: An 8T dead-ended shed, located at TQ37138646 and constructed in sheeting on a steel frame with a sheeting-clad flat roof.

Building 2: A 3T dead-ended repair shop, located at TQ37238648 and constructed in similar fashion to Building 1.

The depot was opened by Eurostar on 2 October 2007.

Operating company in 2010: Eurostar

Allocation: Home base for Class 373 fleet

The servicing shed at Temple Mills depot, under construction on 9 April 2006.   *Philip Stuart*

THORNTON YARD

Strathore Road, Thornton KY1 4DL

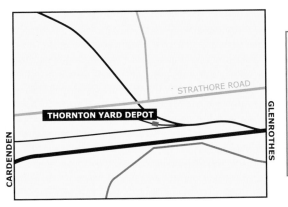

The yard is visible from the line

Directions from Glenrothes with Thornton station:
Leave the station by the approach road, turn right along Main Street and left into Strathore Road. The depot entrance is a drive on the left-hand side at Redford.
(Distance approx 1.9 miles)

A 2T through-road shed, located at NT26339705 and constructed in corrugated sheeting on a steel frame with a corrugated sheeting-clad single-pitched roof. It was opened by BR on 11 October 1984 to replace Dunfermline Townhill and closed in 1992. It was re-opened by EWS in 1996 to service shunters and visiting locomotives.
Operating company in 2010: DB Schenker
Allocation: Nil

The east end of Thornton Yard depot, viewed on 24 July 2003.

Philip Stuart

TOTON

Toton Sidings, Long Eaton, Nottingham NG10 1HS

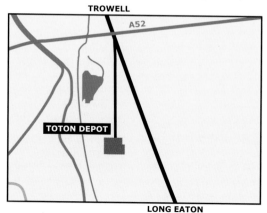

The yard is visible from the line

Directions from Attenborough station: Turn right outside of the station along Attenborough Lane, left into Barratt Lane and left at the end along Nottingham Road. Turn right into High Road and continue along Stapleford Lane and Toton Lane. In Stapleford turn left into New Eaton Road and left at the end along Brookhill Street. Continue along Derby Road, cross the railway bridge and the depot entrance is on the left.
(Distance approx 5.1 miles)

A 16T shed with four through roads, located at SK48473541 and constructed of brick and corrugated sheeting on a steel frame with a glazed and corrugated sheeting-clad transverse multi-pitched roof. It was opened by BR in 1964 and a 5T extension and lifting shop was added at the north end by EWS in 1997.

Operating company in 2010: DB Schenker

Allocation: Home base for Class 60, 66 and 67 fleets

The north end of Toton depot, viewed on 18 February 2004 and showing No 37 895 heading a row of Class 37 locomotives parked in front of the five road extension added in 1997.

Chris Milner

TYNE YARD

DB Schenker, Smithy Lane, Lamesley, Gateshead NE11 0EX

The yard is partially visible from the line

Directions from Dunston station:
Turn right outside of the station into Forge Road and left at the end into Ellison Street. Turn left into Wilson Street, continue along Cypress Crescent and turn left into Maple Avenue. Turn right into Knightside Gardens, left along Woodburn Gardens and left into Whickham Highway. Turn left at the roundabout along Lobleyhill Road, right into Beechwood Gardens, left into Elmwood Gardens, right into Oakwood Gardens and left into Pinewood Gardens. Turn right at the end along Coach Road and continue left along Banesley Lane. Bear right (5th exit) at the roundabout, continue into Lamesley and turn left into Smithy Lane. The depot entrance is on the right.
(Distance approx 4.2 miles)

A 2T through-road shed, located at NZ25575768 and constructed in brick, glazed panels and corrugated sheeting, with a glazed and corrugated sheeting-clad single-pitch gable roof.

It was opened by BR on 28 June 1963 but by the mid-1980s it was only in use for wagon repairs. The depot re-opened on 4 September 1994 to replace Blyth Cambois and in 1997 a 1T through-road fuelling shed, constructed in corrugated sheeting with a single-pitch roof, was added at the southeast corner by EWS. A 2T wagon works was built along the west side in 1999 and by 2010 the depot was used for servicing shunters, visiting locomotives and Class 220 and 221 units for XC.

Operating company in 2010: DB Schenker
Allocation: Nil

The north end of Tyne Yard depot, viewed on 20 August 1989.　　　*Philip Stuart*

VICTORIA GROSVENOR

Grosvenor Road, London SW1V 4BE

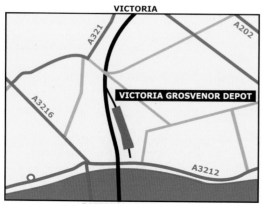

The yard is visible from the line

Directions from Victoria station:
Turn right outside of the station along Wilton Road, right into Warwick Way and the depot is on the left.
(Distance approx 0.6 miles)

A 9T through-road shed, located at TQ28757813 and constructed in corrugated sheeting on a steel frame with a corrugated sheeting-clad triple-pitched gable roof. It was opened by the SR as a carriage shed and used as an EMU depot by BR following electrification in 1960. In 2010 it was in use to service Class 375, 465 and 466 units.
Operating company in 2010: South Eastern
Allocation: Nil

Looking north at Victoria Grosvenor depot on 4 July 1989 with units Nos 1615, 466 021 and 465 169 in view.

Philip Stuart

WARRINGTON
Slutchers Lane, Warrington WA1 1NA

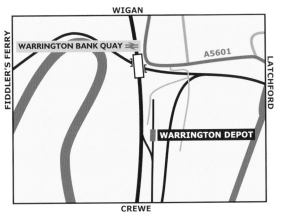

The yard is visible from the line

Directions from Warrington Bank Quay station:
Go straight ahead outside the station into Wilson Patten Street and turn right into Slutchers Lane. Turn first right and the depot is along this road, on the left.
(Distance approx 750yd)

A 2T through-road shed, located at SJ60068748 and constructed in corrugated sheeting on a steel frame with a corrugated sheeting-clad single-pitched roof. It was opened by EWS in May 1997 and in 2010 was used to service Class 66 locomotives.
Operating company in 2010: DB Schenker
Allocation: Nil

Warrington depot, viewed on 7 August 2000 with EWS Class 37 No 37 427 in the shed yard.
Philip Stuart

WASHWOOD HEATH
Common Lane, Birmingham B8 2UW

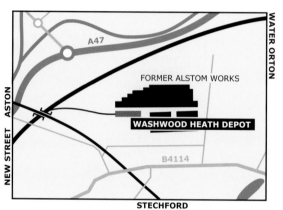

The yard is not visible from the line

Directions from Aston station:
Cross Lichfield Road into Holborn Hill and continue along Aston Church Road. Cross the railway bridge and turn left into a private road. Pass under a railway bridge and the entrance is a gate on the right-hand side.
(Distance approx 0.9 miles)

A 3T dead-ended shed located at SP10348901 and constructed in corrugated sheeting on a steel frame with a glazed and corrugated sheeting-clad single-pitch gable roof. It is part of the main factory of the former Metropolitan Cammell Carriage and Wagon Co which was purchased by GEC Alsthom (later Alstom) in May 1989 and subsequently sold for industrial development in 2002. The site was leased back to Alstom, which ceased operations in 2005.

Operating company in 2010: Hanson Traction
Allocation: Home base for Hanson Traction fleet.

The west end of Washwood Heath depot on 29 July 1993 when it was part of the GEC Alsthom Works complex. The building in use in 2010 as the Hanson Traction depot is the white corrugated sheeting-clad shed in the centre of the picture, seen here surrounded by newly constructed Eurostar and Class 466 rolling stock.
Philip Stuart

WEMBLEY BRENT
Pendolino Way, London NW10 0RP

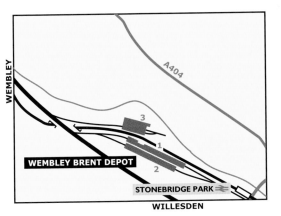

The yard is partially visible from the line

Directions from Stonebridge Park station:
Turn left outside of the station along a private drive and first left under a railway bridge. This leads to the depot (Distance approx 200yd)

Building 1: A 4T through-road shed, located at TQ19218440 and constructed in brick, glazed panels and corrugated sheeting on a steel frame with a glazed and corrugated sheeting-clad single-pitched roof.

Building 2: A 2T through-road shed, located at TQ19208436 and constructed in the same fashion as Building 1.

Both of these buildings were constructed by BR in the 1960s to accommodate electric locomotives and LHCS. In 2010 they were in use as a servicing depot for Class 390 units and Caledonian sleeper stock.

Building 3: A 9T brick-built shed, located at TQ19118453 and constructed with two 2T dead-ended bays, one 4T dead-ended bay (roofless) and a 1T through-road section (partially roofless). Otherwise the buildings have a glazed and corrugated sheeting-clad single-pitched roof. It was originally known as Stonebridge Park and constructed by the LNWR as an EMU depot. It was converted to a heavy repair shop after 1986.

Operating company in 2010: Alstom for Virgin West Coast

Allocation: 1 x Class 08 shunter as depot pilot for Building 3

A publicity shot of Wembley Brent depot with GBRf Class 66 locomotives Nos 66 727, 66 726, 66 725, 66 724 and 66 723 lined up outside Building 3 on 8 January 2007. *Chris Milner*

WEMBLEY CHILTERN

South Way, Wembley HA9 0HD

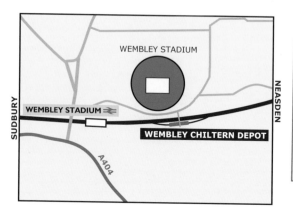

The yard is visible from the line

Directions from Wembley Stadium station: Turn right outside of the station and right along South Way. Proceed around the south side of Wembley Stadium, and the depot entrance is on the right via a railway bridge.
(Distance approx 700yd)

A 2T through-road shed located at TQ19468532 and constructed in sheeting on a steel frame with a sheeting-clad shallow Dutch barn-style roof. It was opened on 2 September 2005 by Chiltern Railways for servicing Class 165 and 168 units.
Operating company in 2010: Chiltern Railways
Allocation: Nil

The east end of Wembley Chiltern depot on 7 September 2005 with unit No.168 002 stabled inside the building.
Chris Milner

WHATLEY

New Frome Quarry, Whatley, Frome, Somerset BA11 3LF

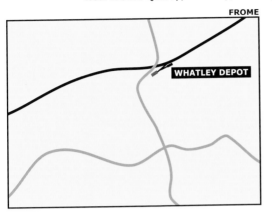

Passenger trains do not operate along this line

Directions from Frome station:
At the end of the station approach road bear left into Wallbridge and then continue along the A362. Bear left into Christchurch Street East, turn right into Wesley Slope and at the roundabout take the first exit along Christchurch Street West. At the next roundabout continue along Broadway and then Egford Hill. Proceed past the junction with Elm Lane, then turn first right and continue into Knaptons Hill. Turn first left and the depot entrance is on the right.
(Distance approx 3.9 miles)

A 2T dead-ended shed, located at ST73314791 and constructed in concrete, glazed panels and corrugated sheeting on a steel frame with a corrugated sheeting-clad single-pitched roof. It was opened in 1990 by ARC and closed in 1993/5 when Mendip Rail took over and concentrated locomotive operations at Merehead. It has since been utilised as a wagon works but may be used as a diesel depot from time to time.

Operating company in 2010: Mendip Rail
Allocation: Nil

Whatley Depot on 26 June 1991 with the T. Hill/Vanguard works shunter *Pride of Whatley* alongside.
Philip Stuart

115

WILLESDEN

Station Approach, Station Road, London NW10 4UY

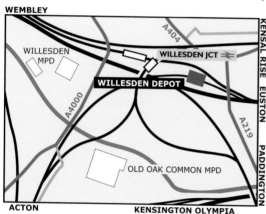

The yard is visible from all of the lines

Directions from Willesden Junction station:
Turn left outside of the station along the approach road and this leads to the depot.
(Distance approx 200yd)

A 6T through-road shed, located at TQ22208283 and constructed in brick and corrugated sheeting on steel frames, with a twin-gable corrugated sheeting-clad and glazed pitched roof. It was opened by BR on 29 March 1965 to service electric and diesel locomotives but later became a multiple-unit depot.

Operating company in 2010: London Overground
Allocation: Home base for Class 150, 313 and 378 fleets

Willesden depot, viewed from Willesden Junction High Level station on 22 March 2004.

Dave McGuire

116

WIMBLEDON PARK

Durnsford Road, London SW19 8DR

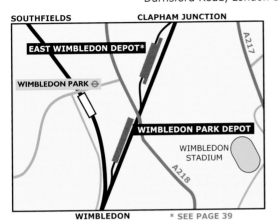

The yard is visible from the line

Directions from Wimbledon Park (LT) Station:
Turn right outside of the station into Arthur Road and right again into Durnsford Road. Continue along the road as it bears right and the depot entrance is at the end of the cul-de-sac.
(Distance approx 500yd)

A 6T dead-ended shed located at TQ25467190 and constructed in corrugated sheeting on a steel frame with a corrugated sheeting-clad twin-pitched gable roof. It was opened in c1936 by the SR and in 2010 was effectively in use to provide additional stabling and servicing for Class 450, 455 and 458 units for the adjacent East Wimbledon depot.
Operating company in 2010: South West Trains
Allocation: Nil

Wimbledon Park depot on 29 April 1989.

Philip Stuart

WOLVERHAMPTON OXLEY

Midlands Traincare Centre, Jones Rd, Oxley, Wolverhampton WV10 6JQ

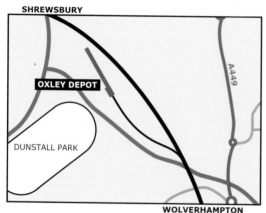

SHREWSBURY

OXLEY DEPOT

DUNSTALL PARK

A449

WOLVERHAMPTON

The yard is visible from the line

Directions from Wolverhampton station: Leave the station along Railway Drive, continue into Fryer Street and turn right into Westbury Street. Proceed along Whitmore Street, turn right into Stafford Street and at the Five Ways Roundabout continue along Stafford Road. Cross the canal, turn left into Jones Road and the depot entrance is on the right-hand side just past the railway viaduct.
(Distance approx 1.4 miles)

A 2T dead-ended shed, located at SJ90580106 and constructed in brick and corrugated sheeting on a steel frame with a corrugated sheeting-clad single-pitched gable roof. It was built on the site of the former Wolverhampton Oxley MPD and opened by BR in 1976. In 2010 it was used for servicing Class 390 units.

Operating company in 2010: Alstom for Virgin West Coast
Allocation: Nil

The south end of Oxley depot, viewed on 28 July 1993.

Philip Stuart

118

YORK LEEMAN ROAD

Leeman Road, York YO26 4XD

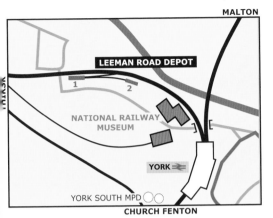

The yard is visible from the line

> **Directions from York station**:
> Turn left out of the station along Station Road, left into Station Rise and left into Leeman Road. The depot entrance is on the right, just past the National Railway Museum.
> (Distance approx 0.7 miles)

Building 1: A 2T through-road fuelling shed, located at SE58895217 and constructed in corrugated sheeting on a steel frame with a partially corrugated sheeting-clad roof.

Building 2: A 1T dead-ended shed, located at SE59195215 and constructed in corrugated sheeting on a steel frame with a corrugated sheeting-clad lean-to roof.

The depot was built in the former shed yard of York North MPD (now the National Railway Museum) and was opened on 10 May 2007 to service Class 185 units.

Operating company in 2010: Siemens for First TransPennine

Allocation: Nil

Building 2 at Leeman Road depot viewed from the southeast.   *Nick Pigott*

LOCOMOTIVE STABLING POINTS

ACTON YARD (DB Schenker) (Photograph on Page 122)
At TQ20338125 on the north side of the line, 0.4 miles west of Acton main line station.

CREWE BASFORD HALL (Freightliner/DB Schenker) (Photograph on Page 123)
At SJ71315346 on the west side of the Stafford line, 0.8 miles south of Crewe station. (The fuelling point and stabling point is on the west side of Basford Hall Yard.)

CREWE DIESEL DEPOT (DB Schenker) (Photograph on Page 123)
At SJ71205426 on the west side of Crewe station. (Locomotives are currently stored here out of use.)

DAVENTRY INTERNATIONAL RAIL FREIGHT TERMINAL (DRS)
At SP57157238 on the north side of the Long Buckby—Rugby line, 4.2 miles east of Rugby station. (A locomotive stables in a headshunt at the very northern end of the DIRFT complex and is visible from the line. There is also a permanent Class 08 at this location, which can normally be seen shunting or stabled in the yard.)

DERBY RTC (Network Rail) (Photograph on Page 124)
At SK36783480 on the south side of the Spondon line, 0.6 miles east of Derby station (opposite Derby Etches Park depot).

DONCASTER STATION
At SE57050298 in sidings on the west side of the station.

DONCASTER ROBERTS ROAD
At SE56560234 on the east side of the Conisbrough line, 0.7 miles south of Doncaster station.

EUSTON STATION (Virgin West Coast) (Photograph on Page 124)
At TQ29488269 between Platforms 15 and 16.

HOO JUNCTION (DB Schenker) (Photograph on Page 125)
At TQ69967352 on the south side of the Gravesend—Strood line, 1 mile northwest of Higham station.

IMMINGHAM DEPOT FUELLING POINT (DB Schenker) (Photograph on Page 125)
At TA19841513 on the southwest side of Immingham Docks. (Although the diesel depot is now closed the fuelling point is still in use.)

INVERNESS MILBURN YARD (DB Schenker)
At NH67504580 near Milburn Junction, on the north side of the line, just east of Inverness station.

IPSWICH STATION (Freightliner) (Photograph on Page 126)
At TM15704374 on the south side of Ipswich station.

MOSSEND YARD (Freightliner/DB Schenker)
At NS74966096 on the east side of Mossend Yard, on the Coatbridge line, 2 miles north of Motherwell station.

NEWCASTLE CENTRAL STATION (East Coast)
Within the station, approximately at NZ24556381.

NEWPORT ALEXANDRA DOCK JUNCTION (DB Schenker)
At ST30338640 on the south side of the Docks branch, on the east side of the Cardiff line, 1.5 miles south of Newport station.

NORWICH STATION
At TG24010823 in adjacent sidings on the south side of the station.

PEAK FOREST (DB Schenker) (Photograph on Page 126)
At SK09227660 at Peak Dale on the west side of the Buxton—Chinley freight line, 5.6 miles southeast of Chinley station.

PLYMOUTH TAVISTOCK JUNCTION (Colas) (Photograph on Page 127)
At SX52365658 on the north side of the line, 1.1 miles east of Plymouth Laira Junction.

PRESTON STATION (Virgin West Coast)
At SD53432916 at the north end of Platform 3.

READING YARD (Freightliner)
At SU69367428 on the north side of the Didcot line, 1.3 miles west of Reading station.

RUGBY STATION (Virgin West Coast)
At SP51307587 at the south end of the station. (A 1T facility, fitted with inspection lights, was opened in the south bay in 2008.)

SALTLEY (DB Schenker)
At SP09218767 on the east side of the Water Orton line, just north of Landor Street Junction. (A DB Class 66, specially modified for banking on the Lickey Incline, stables between duties on a short stub, all that remains of the former diesel depot.)

TAUNTON FAIRWATER YARD (Freightliner)
At ST21502561 on the south side of the Exeter line, 0.6 miles west of Taunton station.

TEES YARD (DB Schenker)
At NZ46361872 on the west side of a road bridge, 0.7 miles east of Thornaby station. Locomotives stable between the freight lines to and from Middlesbrough.

TONBRIDGE PW DEPOT (Colas Rail) (Photograph on Page 127)
At TQ59124595 in the fork of the Ashford and Tunbridge Wells lines, 600yd east of Tonbridge station.

TONBRIDGE WEST YARD (GBRf)
At TQ58004612 on the north side of the Redhill line, 0.5 miles west of Tonbridge station.

TRAFFORD PARK FREIGHT TERMINAL
At SJ80309601 on the north side of the Deansgate line, 0.7 miles east of Trafford Park station.

WELLINGBOROUGH YARD (GBRf)
At SP90436972 on the east side of the Kettering line, 1.1 miles north of Wellingborough station.

WEMBLEY YARD (Freightliner/DB Schenker)
At TQ19418409 on the north side of the Euston line, east of Wembley Central station.

WOLVERTON WORKS (Railcare) (Photograph on Page 128)
At SP81304130 on the northeast side of the works, to the west of Wolverton station.

WORKSOP (Freightliner/DB Schenker) (Photograph on Page 128)
At SK575802 (centre point between the two yards) on the south side of the line, west of Worksop station.

NB: This brief list is not claimed to be comprehensive. In recent years the situation has been fluid to say the least, and some SPs go in and out of use depending on traffic flows. Some of the sites that have been used at some stage in recent years but were out of use for locomotives at the beginning of 2010 are: Bletchley Downside, Gloucester, Healey Mills, Leicester, Motherwell, Old Oak Common (DBS), Stafford station, Temple Mills (DBS) and Thornaby.

ACTON YARD SP

EWS Class 66 No 66 097 parked at Acton Yard stabling point on 1 August 1989.   *John Hillmer*

CREWE BASFORD HALL SP

Freightliner Class 66 No 66 609 at the fuelling point at Crewe Basford Hall stabling point on 7 April 2006. *Nick Pigott*

CREWE DIESEL DEPOT

Crewe Diesel depot, viewed on 7 April 2006. It was opened by BR in 1958, extended in 1964 upon the closure of Crewe North MPD and closed by EWS in December 2003. It remained redundant for a number of years but in 2010 was in use to house stored locomotives. *Nick Pigott*

DERBY RTC

Derby Railway Technical Centre was built by BR to centralise all its research and development activities from across the country. It was opened in May 1964 and consisted of a number of laboratories and office blocks as well as the Research Test Hall. Following the demise of BR it was closed and most of the site let out as the RTC Business Park, but the 4T building and yard was retained by Network Rail to house its sundry collection of locomotives and units. The building and an HST unit are viewed on 7 September 2006. *Chris Milner*

EUSTON STATION SP

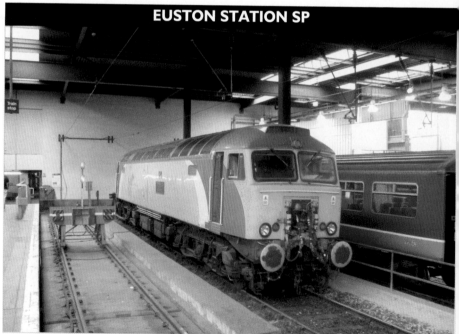

Virgin Trains Class 57 No 57 310 *Kyrano* parked at Euston station SP on 3 July 2009. *Nick Pigott*

HOO JUNCTION SP

Hoo Junction SP looking east on 14 April 2006 with two EWS Class 66 locomotives, Nos 66 084 and 66 072 in view on the left. *Philip Stuart*

IMMINGHAM DEPOT FUELLING POINT

With the docks adjacent, Immingham was provided with a large engine shed, both in steam and diesel days. The latter opened in 1965 but by 2010 all that remained in use was Immingham depot fuelling point and a number of stabling sidings. This view was taken on 9 July 2008. *Nick Pigott*

IPSWICH STATION SP

A diesel stabling and fuelling facility was established on the south side of Ipswich station when Ipswich diesel depot closed in 1968. During the 1970s it was allocated the code IP by BR, and Ipswich SP was still very active on 26 June 2009 as this view of Freightliner Class 66 locomotives Nos 66 530, 66 567, 66 502 and 66 516 shows. *Nick Pigott*

PEAK FOREST SP

Peak Forest SP, viewed on 2 August 2000. This location became a train crew depot following the closure of Buxton diesel depot on 12 October 1997. *Philip Stuart*

The permanent-way depot at Tavistock Junction with Class 09 No 09 013 parked alongside on 27 July 1997. *Philip Stuart*

TONBRIDGE PW DEPOT

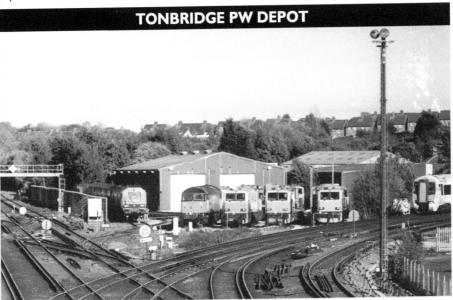

Colas Rail's Tonbridge permanent-way depot was built on the site of the former Tonbridge MPD which closed to steam on 17 June 1962 and was then used as a diesel stabling point until the 1970s. As well as housing track machines, it was utilised as a base for Colas locomotives, and on 25 April 2009 Class 47 No 477 39 was stabled in the yard. *Philip Stuart*

WOLVERTON WORKS

Class 08 No 08 629 stabled at the east end of Wolverton Works on 3 October 2009. This is one of the two Class 08s, the other is 08 649, used for shunting duties here by Railcare. *Dave McGuire*

WORKSOP SP

Part of Worksop SP, viewed on 13 May 1978 with a typical line-up of Class 20, 31 and 47 locomotives stabled adjacent to the 3T wagon works. Although the coal industry has been decimated in the area there is still more than enough traffic to warrant its continuance in use as a stabling point.
John Hillmer